Educated at Narberth
and Reading Universit
went on to post-gra   .....g in
Clinical and Educational Psychology at
the Osnaburgh Clinic, London. He worked
briefly as Clinical Psychologist, St Saviours
Hospital, Jersey, and also taught in special
schools in London. Finally, the author has
spent twenty-four years as an Educational
Psychologist in Norfolk.

... ...

Understanding Child Intelligence

A Unique Guide to Children's Learning Disabilities

PETER LAWRENCE

Robinson Publishing
London

Robinson Publishing
11 Shepherd House
5 Shepherd Street
London W1Y 7LD

First published in 1988
by United Writers Publications Ltd., Cornwall

Published by Robinson Publishing in 1989

Cover illustration courtesy
Horizon International Creative Images

This book is sold subject to the condition that it shall not,
by way of trade or otherwise, be lent, resold, hired out or
otherwise circulated without the publisher's prior
consent in any form of binding or cover other than that in
which it is published and without a similar condition
including this condition being imposed on the
subsequent purchaser.

ISBN 1 85487 044 0

Printed by Wm. Collins & Sons Ltd., Glasgow

ACKNOWLEDGEMENTS

The author would like to acknowledge the help of a number of ex-colleagues and friends who contributed in different ways to the writing of this book. Among them are: Dr Adrian Caro, Beth Corston, Eddie Harvey, Peter Johnston, Dr Brian Lawfield, Margaret Raines, Brian Rumsey, Robert Thomson and Wendy Wigg. And the girls: Lynn Bentley, Joy Lambert, Lesley Pitts and Gill Tuck for managing to type from an alarming variety of script.

Finally, to Kitty, a special thank you for her special kind of help.

Items reproduced from Form L–M of the Stanford-Binet Intelligence Scale by kind permission of NFER-NELSON, Windsor, England.

Extracts from *School Learning Mechanisms and Behaviour* by R.J. Riding, reproduced by kind permission of Open Books, 1980, Somerset, England.

For
Jane, David
and
Daniel

CONTENTS

O.L. Zangwill FRS

It is to Prof. Oliver Zangwill that I owe most in gratitude in connection with the writing of this book.

From our earliest discussions, he made it clear that the project was close to his heart and, in his words, 'long overdue'. His encouragement, quiet wisdom and enthusiasm were constant, and it was always understood that he would write a foreword to the book. This was something which I know he looked forward to doing with much pleasure as I, in turn looked forward to with a keen sense of pride.

We were not to know that before the book was finished he would suffer the stroke which would so severely incapacitate him and so cruelly diminish the quality of his life.

Though he will not read these words, the book stands with many more considerable testimonies to his life as a scholar, teacher and friend.

INTRODUCTION

When I first started to write this book it was my intention
to call it 'My Boy Isn't Stupid' because a mother had recently
used just those words when discussing her child. It was an
expression of frustration from someone who knew that her
son's inability to learn to read was not due to dullness or lack
of effort on his part, nor to indifference or neglect on her
part or the part of his teachers.

My own concern for the plight of such parents and
children, as well as their teachers prompted me to write a
short paper on the subject addressed to my colleagues.* It
was mainly a critique of the voluminous literature on the
subject of dyslexia and was supported by the results of a
survey of one year's work in my own area. Out of this
exercise and my discussions with many parents and teachers
came a decision to try to reach a wider readership, with three
main aims in view. Firstly to offer some reassurance to
parents in this situation that many of us involved professionally share the belief that a failure to learn is frequently
associated with specific factors rather than with low general
ability; secondly, to discuss how these factors are often
associated with defects in the perceptual processes concerned
in formal learning — those of auditory and visual perception —
and, thirdly, to consider the nature of concepts such as
intelligence, perception and learning in a way that would be
intelligible to the majority of parents.

*Appendix I

13

Although the mother's words were an assertion about her boy's intelligence they were also a plea for help and begged many questions. For this reason I have changed the title to 'Understanding Child Intelligence' and written it in a mainly question and answer form. I have also retained the use of the masculine pronoun in the text which, while I trust it will offend no sensibilities, is consistent with the fact that of the population of learning disabled children (of this type), about two thirds of these unfortunates are male.

I am aware that a lot of people find the word disability emotive and undesirable, but I defend my use of it on purely logical grounds. My use of the term disability does imply some underlying pathology (a neurological or physiological defect) however minor in degree, as distinct from the complex of social and emotional factors which are implied by the use of the general term, difficulty. Social and emotional factors can include poor or inadequate care in the home (including inadequate experience and lack of stimulation), poor general health, poor teaching, as well as a wide range of lesser handicaps which inevitably would affect the performance of any child. No one would wish to claim that these factors do not adversely affect general development and educational progress: they are bound to have an effect. I am concerned only to establish that in many instances they are not the primary factors though, obviously, they will exacerbate any such problem as does exist.

If, as is sometimes the case, these extraneous factors are regarded as primary, we are confronted with many anomalies, such as the single sibling with a learning problem in an otherwise successful family; the success of teachers with the majority of children and abject failure with others; the good general adjustment of some of these children (suffering these disabilities) compared with their successful peers and, more significantly perhaps, the fact that some severely mentally handicapped children master the skill of mechanical reading without much difficulty.

It is my contention that many of the so-called difficulties

which are ascribed to this variety of environmental factors and influences are, in their nature, essentially disabilities, and that they should be seen and treated in this light.

It must be significant that after years of intensive activity and debate, controversy still rages around the subject of dyslexia. It is not difficult therefore to understand the despair and frustration of parents when others, presumably more enlightened and in direct contact with the problem, are in disagreement: about its nature, its diagnosis, its remediation, or, even, about whether or not such a condition exists.

One of the chief areas of contention and argument is that of diagnosis. Many medically qualified people who have an interest or who are actively involved with the problem see it as the province of the doctor: specifically the neurologist. This contributes both to the confusion and to the anxiety of concerned parents, leading them as it does to having ideas that there is something medically or physically wrong with their children which, in turn, implies that this is also the direction in which to look for treatment or help. The simple truth is that, though the disability has its roots or origin in some kind of neurological or physiological pathology (however mild), the problem itself is one of behaviour: specifically one of learning. This is the province of the teacher and the psychologist: and it is also the responsibility of psychologists and teachers to identify these problems and to provide the appropriate remedial help.

Current efforts by some local education authorities are designed to deal with dyslexia as a separate, identifiable problem in education. Such measures are often the direct result of pressure groups in the community — with all of whom one can but sympathise. Unfortunately, it is possible that the premises on which these programmes are based are sometimes false, making such efforts inappropriate and, in some cases, likely to make an already difficult situation worse. Such a state of affairs is reminiscent of the days of secondary selection and, in time, the situation could be just as unsatisfactory, with some authorities freely labelling children dyslexic and making substantial provision for them, while others would be less disposed to diagnose the condition and be more conservative in their general readiness to offer any special help.

I say this because the conception of specific learning disabilities as something narrow, and affecting a small number of children is wrong.

If specific learning disabilities of constitutional origin exist — and most responsible authorities would now agree that they do — then, logically, they must occur without reference to a child's social situation or intellectual status.

What does differ — and it is a difference of definitive importance and significance — is the degree to which individual children are affected, irrespective of their general ability level or intelligence. The intelligent child will cope with a minor disability with ease and it could well pass unnoticed: the same problem could be a significant handicap to one less able. At the other end of the scale, a severe disability could seriously impede the progress of the most intelligent individual and could totally defeat the slow-learner.

Failure to give sufficient regard to this is what causes some children to be deemed dyslexic when they most certainly are not, and others to be overlooked or dismissed when there may be a good case to be made that they are.

The argument that if these disabilities occur in less able children they cannot be isolated and identified because their general handicap obscures the issue and makes this impossible, simply does not hold. It is perfectly possible to identify the existence of inadequate perceptual capacities in some less able children — in which case they are doubly handicapped — just as it is possible to show that some of these children, though dull, are highly efficient learners. Certainly, many of them are early and impressive readers, which makes baseless any assumption that this skill is dependent upon average or better intelligence.

It is important that this sizeable population of children

who are affected by specific learning disabilities is not overlooked. They are handicapped in the formal learning situation as surely as others — with physical disabilities — are handicapped on the playing-field.

Instead of recognising that there are degrees of disability which occur in children irrespective of their intellectual status, the term dyslexia has been made increasingly selective — and on the basis of increasingly arbitrary criteria. This is how the trouble began, and continues to contribute to the present confusion.

The lesson to be learned from its unfortunate history is that there is now no logical or defensible way that the term dyslexia can be further contorted to include within it the wide range and variety of constitutionally based learning disabilities which occur. Absurd linguistic and semantic distortions have already been made in an effort to make it a suitably generic term under which all such disabilities can be subsumed and, if they are continued, these efforts can only result in further confusion and be counter-productive. The term has more than outlived its usefulness and, while it was originally conceived in good faith and presented as a cause of learning failure in the acquisition of literacy — in a narrow sense — it has become, with the discovery of an increasing number of such disabilities, a veritable rag-bag of ills which, in comparison, would make Pandora's Box as benign and innocent as a child's gift on Mother's Day.

Perhaps the worst consequence of our ignorance and mismanagement of the situation is the case of the child who, on the basis of all common sense observation is 'bright', and whose parents feel justified in expecting and requiring from him a school performance commensurate with his apparent ability level. When he fails to measure up to these expectations (often compounded by such comments as 'could do better'), he is deemed by his parents to be responsible for his failure — through lack of effort — and has their opprobrium to add to his frustration and burden of misery.

Running him a close second is the child who, though no dullard, is also no scholar and is perhaps of just average ability. If he has caring but also ambitious parents their expectations for him can be unrealistic, and here perhaps the most michievous usage of the term dyslexia comes into its own. Having heard the term, his parents will convince themselves and then proceed to move heaven and earth to convince others — teachers, administrators, not to mention the poor child himself — that, but for a failure on the part of those responsible for his education to recognise his true situation and needs, he could readily scale the academic heights and distinguish himself in a chosen career.

Another unhappy consequence is the converse of this, where some parents believe their children to be failing because they are dull. I have actually had parents say to me that they were aware that their child was no scholar, often following this up with, "Of course, I was no good at school myself". It comes as something of a shock to such parents when you respond to this by telling them that, in fact, their child is intelligent and is failing to learn for quite different reasons.

Lastly, there is the child who again, by any standards is 'bright', and demonstrates this in countless aspects of his general behaviour, but who is failing at school. His parents know that he is motivated, hard working and, in some cases, acutely frustrated through his lack of progress. Unfortunately — but again understandably — because of our wrong thinking about the subject, his particular teachers take the most simplistic view, that he must be dull. If he is trying hard, if they are able and conscientious teachers — and he is still failing — then he must be less intelligent than he appears to be, and than his parents claim for him.

Perhaps, gradually, the situation is improving and teachers are beginning to feel less threatened by these experiences. But there can be no doubt that, due to a lack of knowledge and insight into such cases (again through no fault of their own), many teachers have elected to interpret the child's failure as due to low general ability, rather than accept the only apparently logical alternative — that the responsibility for his failure lies with themselves.

The time has surely arrived when, in fairness to teachers, parents and particularly to children, we should accept the existence of constitutionally based learning disabilities of varying degree as a fact of life, and be prepared to examine and make provision for each one on its own merits. To make reference to some ambiguous concept or standard (such as dyslexia) in order to determine whether or not a child is in need of and deserving of some extra-ordinary and unproven provision is both educationally unsound and morally indefensible.

How can your child be intelligent but a poor learner? Is he perhaps not intelligent after all? Or is it our understanding and use of the word intelligence which is wrong? This apparent paradox is the reason for starting with a discussion of functional or operational intelligence — as opposed to an abstract concept — and which should help to make sense of an otherwise, for many parents, incomprehensible situation.

Does your child have efficient auditory and visual perception — the two most important factors on which successful formal learning — particularly in the early years — depends?

It is wrong to think of these perceptual abilities as 'skills' — as they are usually referred to — which implies a degree of learning, and we should instead think of them more as capacities of a 'given' rather than an acquired nature. Capacities upon which the development of efficient perceptual skills depends. As will be discussed in the text, they certainly appear to be very resistant to training, which would support this view. In fact, these capacities — particularly those required for dealing with symbolised information or the 'written' word — are of such recent origin in evolutionary terms that the simplest biochemical aberration might be all that identifies the fortunate from the unfortunate in this sense. This would go some way towards explaining their apparently extreme vulnerability, as well as the paradox of the intelligent illiterate alongside the dull child who can read.

In attempting to offer a simplified explanation of perception or, more correctly, the processes of perception in a form intelligible to ordinary parents I am aware of the pitfalls of over-simplification. At the same time I do believe that parents have a right to some knowledge of what it is that professionals are talking about, particularly when the object of discussion is their own child.

Many of the more minor problems — while still being disabilities on the definition I have used — have been and are being treated with insufficient regard to their nature. If it works then no harm is done. The harm comes when the problem is not such a minor one and when sometimes deep-rooted prejudice disallows the consideration of an alternative view. In turn this causes wrong assumptions to be made about home environments, parents' attitudes, children's general ability levels, teachers' competence and, above all, to the approach and measures to be adopted in helping a particular child.

I would repeat, I have used the term disability intentionally, as implying the existence of some constitutional factor, however small, and whether innate or acquired. This is an important distinction and needs to be fully understood.

In the long and confused history of the term dyslexia it has sometimes been implied, even directly stated, that there is a genetic component: that is that some genetic defect has been transmitted from one generation to another (most frequently from father to son). There is evidence that such cases exist — I have met them in my own professional life — but I believe they constitute only a minority. Such individuals then, would have a disability which is undoubtedly constitutional and which, additionally, is genetic and innate.

By far the larger group having specific learning problems with a constitutional basis are those whose neurological or physiological defects have not been transmitted by a parent, but who have acquired them during the course of their own development. In general it is an open question whether this refers to a condition or event which occurred before, during or after birth. On the other hand there are individual cases where the evidence points strongly to something which can be identified as possibly significant. Many illustrative cases could be given and typical examples are included in the chapter on case histories.

This group then, which I believe to be very much larger in the population of learning-impaired children than is currently recognised, have disabilities frankly constitutional in character, which are associated with events in their own pre-natal, natal or perinatal histories and are not, in any sense, inherited. These events are not always identifiable and there may well be cases where the abnormality has simply intruded in the course of an otherwise normal development.

A further, equally important aspect of these conditions has to be discussed and understood. As was mentioned earlier, some people find the use of the term disability undesirable for the reasons I have given. This is completely understandable: no one would wish to think of a learning problem being associated with a constitutional defect if it could be explained in terms of poor teaching or inadequate learning opportunities. However, this is primarily an emotional resistance and is one of the factors preventing us coming to terms with the situation and dealing with it in a more objective way.

When the description constitutional is used, it does not need to imply some massive neurological lesion in the child's brain into which you could put your fist. The brain is such a complex organ in its structure, and even more complex in its function, that these defects need not be seen as associated with physical lesions of any kind, but should be thought of in purely functional terms. This will be discussed in more detail in the text but, as this is such an emotive subject, it is as well to stress at the outset that we are not considering damaged brains as such, but often intact and very efficient brains which have difficulty in processing and dealing with certain types of learning material.

There is a great deal that can be done to help these children without recourse to revolutionary measures or to the beguiling prospect of 'special' provision outside the mainstream of education. What these children need is not highly specialised provision available only in some esoteric clinical setting, but the frequent attention of a competent remedial teacher — as is to be found in many ordinary schools.

No one would wish to claim that present provision is adequate, but its deficiencies have to be seen in terms of organisation rather than in terms of failure to provide highly specialised help. What the ordinary school remedial teacher lacks is sufficient access to these children. What the children need is time. Time to achieve in the long term what their non-disabled peers acquire with such apparent ease.

The advent of the 1981 Education Act is timely and one of its most significant and welcome effects will be to ensure that better provision for children with special educational needs will be available in the normal school.

It should be made clear that in this book I am deliberately and mainly concerned with factors affecting intelligible, mechanical reading in a specific sense. There are undoubtedly other frustrating handicaps which inhibit normal educational progress — such as poor spelling or laborious and illegible hand-writing. (This is dysgraphia and should be described as such. It is not always associated with poor reading and its inclusion within the term dyslexia is one of many causes of confusion.) My concern is chiefly with problems associated with the acquisition of the decoding skill, (intelligible mechanical reading), on the grounds that if a child has this skill he is not cut off from the learning situation in a way or to a degree which is likely to threaten his educational achievement significantly in the long-term. It is when he is denied useful access to the written word that his potential for educational progress is severely curtailed. He can 'get by' as a poor speller, or as an indifferent encoder (writer), but, as a non-reader he is doomed, if not to failure, then to a standard of performance and achievement far below what he could achieve as a fully literate individual.

What it comes down to in the end is that in spite of past and current efforts to come to grips with the problem, there is continuing confusion in the minds of parents and among those who are concerned with it in their working lives. This confusion is not due to a lack of will or ability, but is a direct result of a basic misconception of the true nature of specific learning disabilities, compounded as it has been through the continued misuse of the term dyslexia. This confusion is likely to remain with us until this ambiguous term is removed, if not from the dictionary then, hopefully, from the vocabulary and usage of all those who are involved in education.

1

WHAT IS INTELLIGENCE?

Introduction

Parents and teachers can be forgiven for equating intelligence with learning ability. This is a commonsense view. To them the intelligent child is the one who learns with apparent ease, gives a good account of himself at examinations and eventually goes on to acquire qualifications and, in the course of time, a good career and standard of life for himself.

Apart from being the commonsense view this is the only view that can be taken of functional or operational intelligence: that is, as we use the term in everyday life — whether as professionals or laymen. The theoretical debate on the nature of intelligence, (which is centuries old), is concerned with it in a philosophical and scientific sense, rather than with its operational significance in real life situations.

A brief historical note is included at the end of this chapter, more as a matter of general interest than as contributing anything to the main objective of this book.

Although psychologists and others have been obliged to tie down the concept, even to attempt to measure it, in order to assess its significance for different aspects of human behaviour and the processes involved in learning in particular, such procedures inevitably give rise to artificial and misleading notions of intelligence as an entity — as a thing in itself. It is, essentially, a quality of behaviour and has no existence in isolation from it. It is more useful to think of it as an adjective, describing behaviour; behaviour can be intelligent or unintelligent: or, as an adverb; people behave intelligently or unintelligently as the case may be.

It is essential to keep this operational view of intelligence in order to avoid the absurdities which result from thinking of it as an entity and, above all, as one that can be measured in immutable terms.

For our purposes it has to be used in its functional or operational sense, as an aspect of behaviour which is observable and employable in the classroom. The question for the teacher will always be, 'Can I teach this child and, if not, why not? Never mind what labels might have been stuck on him but, can I teach him?'

A major thesis of this book is that the answer to this question is not always a straightforward one, nor one to be dismissed lightly.

Some teachers, as a result of their experience, have long ago rejected the idea of a simple one to one correspondence between ability and achievement, and are profoundly puzzled by some of the apparent contradictions they meet. It is becoming clear to them that some of our old-established ideas of equating intelligence with learning ability, or problem-solving behaviour have to be revised and due recognition given to the fact that formal learning — and, in particular, learning at different levels — is not dependent in a direct way upon a child's reasoning ability but, rather upon certain specific perceptual capacities which have a special significance for learning.

This means that a child can be capable of one kind of intelligent behaviour but not another.

I am sure you are acquainted — perhaps parents especially — with the child who can, for example:

. . . make complicated models of aeroplanes, ships, etc.
— following complex plans or blue-prints visually.
. . . repair and maintain mechanical vehicles — even take an engine down and put it back together again.
. . . look after livestock (sometimes his own, if he is

lucky) on his father's farm, including all aspects of their management right up to marketing them and making a profit.

. . . do electrical work (perhaps illegally) around the house, including adding new circuits, making repairs to gadgets — from toasters to washing-machines and radios.

. . . create impressive disco set-ups with elaborate visual and audio components and managing these enterprises so as to realise a sizeable income and profit for themselves.

Yet, all the while, these children can be failing at school: frequently illiterate and often achieving little in the way of number work. What they do achieve is all done laboriously and with great effort.

Are these children dull?

The great divide it seems is between being able to deal with or not being able to deal with symbolic material. If there were no such thing as writing, the intelligent child would surpass his less able peers all the time. But this is not the way things are. It is a fact of life that a great deal of our knowledge resides in books and cannot be wrested from them without an ability to read.

This has implications for a child's functional intelligence, including his assessed IQ.

Although we now know that it is wrong to regard the Intelligence Quotient as something immutable and unchanging, it is not widely realised to what extent — and even less why this is the case.

If a child's intelligence is assessed when he is quite young — say at four or five years (there can be a variety of clinical or educational reasons for doing this), he may well demonstrate that he possesses to an acceptable or even impressive degree the basic skills which are commonly included in test batteries for this age group. These could include such things as: manipulating objects; erecting structures with bricks; repeating words or phrases; copying simple figures — like a circle or square; doing jig-saw type problems and so on.

If his performance is average or better for his age, he will get a correspondingly 'good' IQ.

In the following years — say from six to nine — he should be developing skills which themselves depend upon capacities not accessible to assessment previously. These are the capacities which are the main point of discussion in the chapter on Perception.

If the child is fortunate and possesses adequate or good perceptual abilities, his intellectual development will follow a relatively even course and he will acquire all the skills and attainments commensurate with his general ability level.

If he is less fortunate, and his perceptual abilities are inefficient or inadequate, he will not easily acquire these skills — upon which a lot of his later learning depends. This is particularly dramatic in the case of reading — but other areas of learning are sometimes affected, either separately or in association with it.

A number of the abilities assessed by IQ tests in these later years are of an abstract nature — as distinct from the concrete nature of the material used in the earlier years — and it is here that the child who, by reason of his inadequate perceptual capacities, is disadvantaged. He might have failed to acquire the skills which, for their successful learning, depend upon relatively intact and efficient perceptual processes.

Thus the situation can arise where a child's effective intelligence — his IQ — is found to be lower than it was some years previously. And it is this fact that points the primacy of perceptual abilities in formal learning.

As will be discussed in the chapter on Learning, there are other important determinants of academic success — particularly at higher levels — but, in the acquisition of the basic skills, the skills on which so much of a child's educational progress is based, these perceptual capacities, and the perceptual abilities which derive from them, are of all but definitive importance.

What are the implications of this view of intelligence for the individual child?

Clearly, if a child has a good brain in the traditional sense, and is additionally fortunate in having efficient perceptual processes at his disposal then, for him, educationally, the sky is the limit.

If he has the good brain, but along with it has perceptual disabilities, he will be handicapped by them as a function of their severity. If, within these limits he is fortunate and these disabilities are slight they will frustrate his progress hardly at all and might well go unnoticed by himself and others. If they are severe, he will be significantly handicapped and there will be definite limits set on what he will achieve. But in his case, because of his powers of reasoning and consequent ability to find 'strategies' and other means of circumventing his difficulties, he will be, to that extent fortunate, and, given the necessary motivation and persistence might well blast his way through to a successful — even professional — career. But, if he achieves this, let no one say, 'There you are, I said all along he had no problem'. His problem did not go away — they don't. And he should be given all credit for his achievement in overcoming it.

The same complementary situation occurs with all levels of general ability on the one hand, and all levels of perceptual disability on the other. The very able or average, with a slight to a severe degree of disability; the below average, with a similar range of disability; right down to the child of limited intelligence who has perceptual disabilities in addition to this, and is, therefore, to be seen as multiply-handicapped.

I hope it is clearer now how a child can be intelligent but a poor learner and, as a result of this fail to meet the expectations of his parents and teachers. Also, let us not forget, his expectations of himself. Many intelligent children who have learning disabilities of a significant degree are as puzzled by their failure — particularly to read — as anyone else. They need above all to be reassured that people understand their predicament and are not holding them responsible for their failure to produce expected results. Parents, especially, are the important people here, as it is often a feeling of 'failing' them, of 'letting them down' that is the cause of the most acute pain to these children. And, while there is no magic wand available with which they might put things right, they can make their child's situation much more tolerable through a sympathetic attitude and readiness to discuss his problem with him. Particularly to show him that, on the one hand they know that his failure does not indicate that he lacks ability and, equally, that they are capable of accepting his scholastic performance on trust. That he is achieving all that it is in his power to achieve, and accepting that this might be below their earlier hopes and expectations of him.

Can intelligence be measured?

When your child has an intelligence test, what happens? What is the psychologist doing or hoping to achieve?

There are a number of different IQ tests in current use — often differing significantly in structure — but all having one feature in common. They assess individual aspects of a child's mental abilities, and for this reason comprise, in a sense, a large number of individual tests. Although the overall performance is expressed in terms of a figure (or IQ) it may have been achieved in quite different ways by different children. Any two children might have widely differing successes and failures among their responses to these different tasks, yet will achieve the same IQ.

Although this may be puzzling to some parents it is, if you think about it, no more than we should expect. In any large community many people could be found to share the same IQ — if they were assessed — yet they will be doing very different things in the way of earning a living, and will have differing interests and life-styles. This is especially true among people in the average range of ability, where will be found technicians, tradesmen, clerical workers, sales people, etc. In fact, they may have little in common in the way of their personalities except that they all happen to share roughly the same IQ.

The important point to be understood here is that the successful completion of one of these individual tasks tells you only one thing: the child can do that task. And it doesn't tell you anything else. It does not tell you that he could do an 'easier' task; nor that he might be able to do a more 'difficult' task.

There are lots of reasons why children have strengths and weaknesses in their mental abilities (some are discussed in the chapter on Perception) and it is wrong to make any assumptions about what these might be in any individual case.

When the child's performance on the test is complete his successes are added together and this (total) result is then set against a standard performance for his age. A standard which will have been established by assessing the performance of many thousands of children on the same scale.

There are two important limiting factors regarding the validity and usefulness of this procedure. Firstly, the sometimes widely differing distribution of successes and failures among children doing the test: secondly, the fact that we can only draw inferences from the child's performance. The performance itself is of little interest: it is what that performance means in terms of the child's potential for learning that has significance.

In regard to the distribution of a child's successes and failures for instance, it is possible for two children to obtain precisely the same IQ, though one of them will have failed on tasks normally within the ability of children well below his age: and, at the same time will have succeeded on tasks normally within the ability of children who are much older. The other child's performance may be significantly different in being a 'well-balanced' performance, with a limited range and distribution of successes and failures.

This can best be explained by reference to the type of test which uses the concept of mental-age, such as the Stanford-Binet. (Though it is important to make the point that the same principle or factor of distribution will apply whatever type of test is used.)

In such a test individual tasks are grouped according to chronological age: six for each year group in this case. Each group representing a standard or average level of performance.

A child — say a ten-year-old — may have a specific cognitive weakness, possibly of perception, which will cause him to fail on a task normally within the competence of a child of six. The same child, because of good reasoning ability, may complete successfully a task which is included in the group at the fourteen year level. Thus his successes and failures range over nine years.

Another ten-year-old — the one with the well-balanced record or range of abilities — may succeed on all the tests at year nine; all but one at year ten; and on three out of six at year eleven. Thus, his successes and failures range over only three years.

When each boy's successes are aggregated together, they achieve the same mental-age of 10 yrs. 3 mths. and, as they are both ten years old, they will obtain the same IQ.

It will be obvious that these widely differing performances will have significant implications for these children, particularly in regard to what they will achieve in formal learning.

We are, of course, discussing a hypothetical situation and, generally speaking, such wide discrepancies between individuals are rare. Also, and more importantly, it is what a child shows himself capable of achieving in the environment of the classroom that matters, not theoretical considerations. As was mentioned earlier, the only question for the teacher is, 'can I teach this child?'

These things become important however, and take on a new significance when the individual child begins to fail, or when his performance falls below reasonable expectations. This is when close examination of a child's true learning

31

situation is desirable, and in no case should facile assumptions be made.

As is discussed in the historical note on the nature of intelligence later in this chapter, the IQ does not imply a measurement of intelligence in any definitive sense. What the test is doing is assessing aspects of behaviour, by setting them against the behaviour of others in similar standardised situations.

Within these limits such assessments have an obvious usefulness in education: so long as results are treated with caution — particularly where there are unusual factors affecting a child's situation — and provided that no unwarranted conclusions are drawn or decisions taken on the basis of this information alone.

What does having a high IQ or low IQ mean?

This question immediately begs a second question: high or low in relation to what?

We have already seen that the information these tests give us refers to standards of behaviour or performance. With a characteristic such as height within any community there will be a distribution from the shortest at one extreme to the tallest at the other and, as observation will show, there will be a majority within an average range, with a decreasing number — falling away in each direction — to a small number who are either very tall, or very short.

We know that in the case of a physical characteristic such as height we could, (theoretically), make exact measures, as well as obtain accurate information about its distribution in the community.

Although when attempting to measure a characteristic of behaviour, (such as intelligence), procedures will be different and results less accurate, the principle of distribution will still apply. There will be a small number who are severely mentally handicapped at one extreme, with a small number of highly gifted people at the other. The majority will again be within an average range.

In the case of the intelligence quotient, the mid-point or average of this range of ability is taken as one hundred — with the extremes ranging from below 30 to above 180. It is arrived at by setting an individual's actual score against the expected or standardised score (for his age group), and multiplying the product by 100. The earlier intelligence tests — some of which, such as the Stanford-Binet, are still widely used — express the individual's actual performance in terms of a mental age, so that the formula then becomes:

$$\frac{\text{Mental Age}}{\text{Chronological Age}} \times 100 = IQ$$

There are certain inherent disadvantages in using the concept of mental age, the greatest being that of assuming any necessary identity between two individuals obtaining the same mental age — other than the fact that they achieved the same score. Clearly the child of eight years who achieves a mental age of ten years and an IQ of $(^{10}/_8 \times 100) = 125$ is, educationally, very differently situated from a child of ten years who achieves the same mental age of eight years and an IQ of $(^{8}/_{10} \times 100) = 80$.

Some more recent tests use the concept of Standard Scores* in place of Mental Ages, which eliminates this particular hazard — but the indications are that use of the concept of the IQ will continue for some time. Hopefully, it will never be quoted without qualification in any given case.

It will be seen from all this that having a low or high IQ is something determined statistically. It is not a measure of some characteristic of the individual per se, but an index of his intellectual function in relation to that of others.

*Standard scores are obtained by establishing the standard or average score obtained on a particular task by a large number of children and setting the individual child's performance against this. Thus it has the additional advantage of indicating the relative level of a child's performance on separate items of a test, rather than on the result as a whole.

It is a widely abused and misunderstood concept — to a lesser degree in education now perhaps — but significantly in law, and, of course, socially.

Having said that, it has an undoubted usefulness in helping to determine the educational needs of individual children and in establishing appropriate educational provision, particularly for the handicapped.

What significance does a child's IQ have for his formal learning: that is, what is the relationship between a child's intelligence and his educability?

Ideally there would always be a very close relationship between a child's assessed intelligence and his ability to learn. In practice this is not the case.

As we discover more about how children learn — and about how they fail to learn — so it becomes increasingly apparent that not only is this relationship a complex one but, also, that there are real dangers in making unwarranted assumptions about it: partly because of our traditional ideas about intelligence and how we go about assessing it, and, partly because of equally unwarranted assumptions about the processes of formal learning itself.

On the face of it there is nothing wildly unreasonable about the expectation that an intelligent child should be able to learn. If a child can obtain a high IQ then surely — given motivation and learning opportunity — he should succeed in learning. If this turns out not to be so, then, there must be a case for looking closely at our established views and procedures.

When the average person thinks about intelligence there is little doubt that what he has in mind is something in the nature of 'reasoning ability'. When he thinks about learning — of any kind, formal or otherwise — he sees the one as naturally and directly dependent upon the other.

And for a great deal of formal learning this is the case. But not for all.

When a child fails to learn — especially to learn to read — this is usually the first direct demand on the child's formal learning ability that means anything to the average parent. If, before this, the child has appeared and behaved as a normal child, the parents' expectation is that his learning will proceed normally. Whatever the demands of 'learning to read', they assume that he has the reasoning ability to meet those demands and, if necessary, to 'reason things out' when a difficulty presents itself.

This is where preconceived and traditional ideas about intelligence and learning begin to fall down. Intelligence or reasoning ability on the one hand, and 'educability' on the other, turn out to be different things.

There are aspects of learning to read that have little to do with reasoning ability. They are dependent upon perceptual processes and, if these are inefficient or defective in a given child's case, no amount of reasoning ability — particularly in the early days of his reading — will avail him a great deal. It will not allow him to 'crack the code' which is the essential requirement for making sense of the written word.

If he does have good general or reasoning ability, then this will certainly help him in dealing with his problem — specifically in helping him to find ways of compensating for any disability and in finding alternative routes to effective perception — in the long term. But there is no question that somehow or other this has to be achieved.

Intelligence can't work until information is available to it in an intelligible form.

It is the extent to which the child can organise sensory information efficiently, and can achieve the highest level of perception of which he is capable, that will determine his efficiency as a learner and, in turn, the extent to which his full educational potential will be realised.

It follows from this that so long as we retain current concepts of intelligence, and methods of assessing it, there will be many cases where there is a significant discrepancy between a child's assessed IQ and what he is able to achieve. It does not mean that some substantial 'error' of assessment has been made. If a child does achieve a high IQ, there can be no doubt that, in these terms he is intelligent. What is not guaranteed is that, equally, he will be an efficient learner. This will be particularly true in the early years if, (because of a perceptual disability), he is involved in an unequal struggle of trying to cope with a situation, (such as learning to read), for which he is ill-equipped. Later when, hopefully, he has attained an adequate standard of literacy, he will be in a position to exploit all of his cognitive skills to the full.

In cases where a child's assessed IQ is lower, precisely the same will obtain. What he will achieve in the way of formal learning in the short-term will equally be dependent upon the same processes of sensory organisation and perception. This is his educability. The other limits set on his ultimate achievement will be determined — as in all cases — by the quality of his brain in a wider sense.

Intelligence then is what a child does with his brain rather than what it is. Intelligence is behaviour, not a biological entity or state.

Can you do anything to raise the level of your child's IQ?

Once again, reference has to be made to the later part of this chapter and the discussion of the nature of intelligence — but, here we are considering specifically a child's IQ. And, as we have seen, this is an index of function in a closely structured situation — not a measure of his functional intelligence in any or all situations.

In the sense that the results of the assessment of this behaviour depend upon the child's success or failure on individual tasks, it follows that by direct concentration on training to meet the demands of these tasks a quite artificial and spurious result can be obtained. Fortunately, fewer children (if any) are now exposed to this sort of 'training' in tackling intelligence tests, but it was not uncommon in the days of selection procedures for secondary education. (Here of course group tests of ability were used so that they could be administered to large numbers of children. In the ordinary way an IQ test is given on an individual basis and has much greater validity.)

I recall one extreme example of this from my own experience when a boy of thirteen was referred to me because of his poor performance in his grammar school. When I carried out a full investigation of his abilities and attainments I discovered that his intelligence level was well below average! It seemed hardly credible that he could have been successful in the selection tests but, later, when discussing the situation at home the explanation was both available and clear.

He was the adopted son of a primary school head-teacher who had seen it as in the boy's interest to get him into grammar school 'at all costs'. Being familiar with the group tests of ability being used, he had tutored the boy over a period of years to a point where his performance on these specific tasks bore very little relation to his actual ability level. Seeing the boy's wretched situation and obvious misplacement he eventually accepted that his efforts, though well intentioned, were misguided and, in the result disastrous.

The validity of any IQ achieved in this manner would be limited and the whole exercise has to be seen as falling into much the same category as teaching a dog to do tricks.

One of the most significant characteristics or features of general intelligence is its generality: that is its competence to meet a wide range of intellectual demands. In this way it contrasts dramatically with a skill which, by definition is mainly specific and learned. Usually the result of developing a single capacity.

It must be stressed that in discussing this 'sort' of intelligence we are discussing an individual's task-oriented performance in a very specific way. As has been seen, it is possible to influence what he will achieve, but only at the cost of sacrificing the validity of the result.

37

Normally a child (or adult) who is being assessed has not been prepared or trained to meet the situation. Therefore the results of the assessment (the IQ) should be related to the individual's ability to cope with a generality of situations.

So the short answer is 'yes', it is possible to raise the level of your child's assessed IQ but, to the extent that he might have been purposefully prepared to meet the demands of the test, then the result will be invalidated.

Is a child's intelligence fixed or can it change over a period of time?

Having seen that intelligence is a matter of behaviour it is obvious that it cannot wholly be determined by genetic factors alone. There must be a range within which the given potential for intelligent behaviour (including aspects of formal learning) of an individual child, will be affected by the quality of the environment — in physical, social, emotional and psychological terms — in which he develops.

The importance of adequate physical provision and care is easy to understand. There is plenty of evidence that neglect in this regard adversely affects all-round health and development and must, in consequence, have significance for the child's intellectual development as well. This has to be viewed with caution however, because such neglect is more often than not associated with other forms of deprivation which could be of equal or greater importance. On the purely physical side there is no evidence that provision over and above what the child needs for normal healthy development has any significant effect.

There is mounting evidence on the other hand that the mother's behaviour and habits during pregnancy can have significant positive and negative effects. In particular the ingestion of too much alcohol and excessive smoking are known to be injurious. On the positive side, looking after her own physical health and maintaining a good life-style can only be beneficial in promoting the baby's healthy all-round development. (There have been claims that procedures aimed at improving the oxygen supply to the unborn baby by applying additional artificial pressure to the mother's abdomen specifically promotes intellectual growth. The verdict on this and similar procedures must remain — for the present at least — unproven.)

The effects of social, emotional and psychological factors are generally so interwoven in a child's environment that — for the purposes of this question — there is little point in trying to separate them out. They, in a sense, comprise all the other influences on his development after his physical situation has been taken into account.

Allowing for the fact that there is excessive enthusiasm from time to time for the significance and importance of particular factors or points of view, there is a tendency for what is good to remain and to gain acceptance, if only in modified form. This is especially true of two aspects of a child's early life experience. One is the quality of the loving care he receives and the degree to which his emotional needs are met; the other is the amount of general attention and stimulation he receives which makes demands on his capacity to understand the world around him.

In both these areas it is the affects of deprivation which are most obvious and which lead us to conclusions regarding their importance.

These are, in themselves, subjects worth study by any parent and this is not the place to pursue them in any detail. On the other hand, it is not inappropriate to emphasise the importance of these aspects of parenthood which, too often are either ignored or, in other instances treated too casually — generally for the reason that their true significance is not understood, rather than because of anything approaching wilful neglect.

In regard to the child's emotional needs, it can be said that his capacity to relate to others — in the early years to his peers and in the longer term to adults — will be largely determined by the quality of the primary social relationships

39

established during the early years of his development. Put rather simplistically, if he discovers that the adults around him are sources of comfort and satisfaction and can also be trusted and relied upon, he will be conditioned to respond to others in a characteristically caring and trusting way. This (obviously) has more direct significance for his psychological well-being than his intellectual growth but, in the sense that this will have significance for all his behaviour, particularly his social and emotional adjustments — it has a relevance for his effective intelligence and potential for learning as well. There is little doubt that the secure, well-adjusted child is better placed to do full justice to himself educationally than the child who is insecure, withdrawn or neurotic.

Although the formative years of nought to five or six are generally accepted as the most important in this respect, it is clear that unfortunate circumstances or life experiences, can have an adverse affect on a child's intellectual functioning well beyond these years.

Drawing on my own experience once again, I well recall seeing a ten-year-old boy whose behaviour was giving his teacher cause for concern during the break-up of his parents' marriage. Although during my first interview with him he was clearly an unhappy child, he was, within these limits, friendly and responsive and, on an intelligence test, obtained an IQ of 120. He was also, at the time, extremely well turned-out, and generally presented as a pleasant, attractive personality.

When I next did a full assessment of his situation after a period of less than two years — during which time his father had left the home and they were in much reduced circumstances — he obtained an IQ of 97. Also, he presented very differently, as an apathetic, uninterested boy who, additionally, was no longer well-dressed and was showing all the signs of living in a very different psychological and social environment.

There is no doubt in my mind that his depressed effective intelligence was a direct consequence of his social situation.

I quote this case only to illustrate how, as behaviour, functional intelligence is vulnerable to, and can be affected by environmental factors to a significant degree.

The merits and significance of a 'stimulating environment' for a child's intellectual development have to be considered very carefully. As with most things it is extremes that should be avoided.

Whereas to most people it is self-evident that a child's developing brain needs a minimal degree of stimulation to promote intellectual growth it is, unfortunately, not so evident to some parents that reasonable limits should be observed in this regard.

In the very early days it is probable that nature herself applies limiting mechanisms which protect the neonate's brain from being overloaded by sensory bombardment — intentional or otherwise. But these limiting mechanisms clearly don't operate indefinitely. Since the idea got around that lack of stimulation in the early years was a primary cause of poor or slow cognitive development some parents have become obsessed with making sure that this will not happen to any child of theirs!

Recent studies show that the very young infant — only hours old — is capable of a degree of discrimination between both auditory and visual stimuli. A degree of learning in fact, which marks the beginning of cognitive development. It is a beguiling prospect — which is proving altogether too attractive to some parents — that giving their child plenty of stimulation at this time is the key to developing a super-brain and, whatever limiting mechanism may be operative in the early months or years, there is a danger that this sort of excessive stimulation of a young child will have unfortunate results.

All development should be seen as essentially a natural process, and any significant departure from this — that is anything approaching a human equivalent to stuffing the crops of the unfortunate geese of Strasburgh in order to produce large livers — should be avoided.

Development should be an all-round process.

Generally speaking, if one aspect of a child's development is intentionally accelerated it can only be done at the expense of another. Thus the child who is over-protected or over-mothered can be excessively fearful and socially inept. Equally, if there is over-concentration on intellectual development, a skewed or unbalanced personality can again result, in whom learning becomes an end in itself, and there is a corresponding lack of emotional awareness and growth.

The aim of responsible parents should be to provide the optimal conditions and opportunities for growth of all kinds.

So the answer once again is yes, the level of a child's effective intelligence can be raised over a period of time — particularly in the early years. But before embarking on any course designed to achieve this, do give some thought to the whole child.

Do intelligent parents always have intelligent children and dull parents always have dull children?

The short answer is no, not in all cases. But in the majority of cases yes, they do.

This is an emotive subject and one which demands serious discussion for that reason alone — particularly as it affects parental attitudes to, and expectations of their children in regard to their educational achievements.

For many people, simple observation of everyday life causes them to conclude that a significant degree of a child's intelligent behaviour is determined by biological or inherited factors, but it should be made clear that where readers are predisposed, for whatever reason, to reject this conclusion, no serious attempt is being made in this book to persuade them to take any different view.

The main difficulty again arises over the question of what we mean by intelligence. What kind of intelligence are we talking about?

In this instance — and only in this instance — we need to set aside the notion of intelligence as behaviour and think of it in terms of the biological and genetic factors which determine it. The idea of inheritance has to be seen in biological terms: any notion of inheriting behaviour is obviously a nonsense.

Whether we think in terms of brain size and structure — the number of nerve fibres and cells and the way they are organised — or in terms of its physiology, the commonsense view must be that there are significant differences between some brains and others. Differences which in a direct way will determine their potential for organising and initiating intelligent behaviour. Analogies, particularly when it comes to anything as complex as the brain are dangerous, but, as in the case of the discussion of perception, it is scientifically tenable to use the crude analogy of the computer. Some computers are bigger and better than others, in the sense that they can handle and process more information. In this very basic and non-functional sense, some brains are bigger and better than others.

The assumption is sometimes made by parents that, as they themselves are not educated to any significant degree and are unable to show evidence of high intelligences — in the nature of their employment or life-style — there is little chance that their children will be any different.

It cannot be overstated that, as we are thinking in purely biological terms in this context, this assumption is wholly unjustified and can be totally wrong. It is just possible, (if somewhat less probable), for the biological potential for high general intelligence to reside in the brain of an unskilled labourer as in the brain of a high court judge, or a distinguished academic. What their children will inherit is not intelligence, but a capacity to develop it.

To refer to my own experience once again, one of the most interesting examples illustrating the genetic aspect of intelligence came through the referral to me of a five-year-old boy by the head teacher of a small village school. He presented a problem purely in terms of his precocious ability and appetite for learning — he was already a fluent reader — and

43

the head was seeking guidance on how to make appropriate provision for him.

At interview the child was all that had been claimed for him in terms of his alertness and responsiveness and I confirmed that he was of very superior ability, with an IQ of 170+. I had already been given basic information about the family who lived in a council house nearby and knew that the father was a lorry-driver.

When I visited the home to discuss the parents' management of the little boy I discovered that yes, his father drove a lorry, transporting carrots for processing from local growers. When I questioned his wife more closely about him, I was not surprised to discover that he was a very frustrated and unfulfilled man. He tried to find satisfaction outside his work through reading scientific journals and watching informative or educational programmes on television.

Some ten years later he is now a self-trained bricklayer and plasterer and has a much happier working life.

The five-year-old is now fifteen and, while clearly not highly motivated is coping with considerable ease in his 'O' level course and has taken some subjects early. When challenged by his mother recently about not doing any revision he pointed to his head, saying that he didn't need to revise . . . 'that's there'.

One of the most celebrated proponents of the inheritance, or capacity theory of intelligence was the late Sir Cyril Burt, who was the first educational psychologist to be employed in this country — by the London County Council. Although, sadly, some of his work has been criticised as dishonest for his apparent misuse of research information and he himself discredited for this reason, it would be foolish if those who dismiss his credibility on these grounds were to dismiss his fundamental premise with the same zeal. (His work is referred to later in the Historical Note.)

As was said earlier, what is inherited is not intelligence, but varying capacities for its development. In this sense, there is a logical probability that the genetic factors which determine these capacities will be transmitted from parents to children in precisely the same way as other characteristics, such as height, a tendency to obesity or blue eyes.

It should again be stressed that where inherited factors are concerned we can only think in terms of probabilities: there is nothing absolute or definitive in the process. One obvious variable is the mix of genes which an individual child will get from his two parents. This is why, in the children of one family you will find wide differences in physical characteristics between them; some conspicuously linked with one parent and some with the other. And this will apply in respect to intelligence as well. It is not uncommon to find quite significant differences in this respect among siblings (both brothers and sisters), particularly in large families. This would be most common where one parent was significantly more intelligent than another but, as observation will show, in our society there is a tendency for like to marry like, so that a wide discrepancy between the abilities of parents would be the exception rather than the rule.

There is one important respect in which this law of probability does not hold. Nature, apparently, does not like extremes. In cases where extremes come together — say two very highly intelligent parents — there is a probability that their offspring will be somewhat less intelligent than they are. Equally, where two parents of very low intelligence have children, there is a probability that their children will be somewhat more intelligent than they are. Scientifically this is known as regression to the mean or, in more ordinary language, a movement toward the average and away from the extremes. It should be stressed that this is again only a statistical concept based on the observation of individual differences in intelligence. The mechanism or process operating makes obvious biological sense in that it avoids extremes becoming more extreme, with predictably disastrous results.

If intelligence is what a child does, how much is determined by subjective factors of the nature of will and motivation?

There is a good chance that what might have been confusing or misleading in the answer to the previous question will be made clearer here, now that we are moving back to the operational concept of intelligence as behaviour: as something a child does with his brain as opposed to what it is. In this sense the question gives us the opportunity of looking at an important aspect of the problem posed by the relationship between the constitutional and behavioural aspects of intelligence.

As free agents, all individuals, both young and old, have an element of choice in what they elect to do. There will be a number of factors affecting this freedom of course, particularly in the early years, but, ultimately, what the individual achieves will largely be determined by his own will, and particularly his desire or lack of desire to attain certain goals.

In the matter of intelligence then, what the individual achieves is not going to have absolute limits set on it by the dimensions and quality of his brain. What he ultimately achieves will depend on the amount of effort he is prepared to put into meeting any given situation. Thus, achievement, as such, should not be taken as a measure of an individual's ability.

In formal learning for instance teachers are always aware of children who achieve a good measure of success with apparently little effort. At the same time they will be aware of others who are achieving roughly the same level of performance, but who are doing so only through significantly more industry and effort.

In the long run it may turn out that the very industrious child — particularly if he has been hardworking from an early age — will not only achieve formal attainments above those of his more indolent peers but, again within limits, could be found to have raised the level of his effective intelligence. He would obtain a higher IQ.

This is why it is essential to hold fast to the concept of intelligence as a quality of behaviour: as something dynamic and having reality only in behaviour.

This is also why the claim that genius is made, and not born, has an element of truth in it. A 'potential' for genius which is not realised is meaningless. There are many ingredients to outstanding achievement and a strong will and sustained effort are not the least of these. It is not at all fanciful to speculate how many more geniuses, or examples of outstanding achievement there might have been if potential was always accompanied by adequate will and effort.

Such things as will and determination are, essentially, matters of character rather than personality. They are very much determined by environment and the influences to which a child is exposed during his development. Economic factors will sometimes apply, where material deprivation will have instilled a resolve in the individual to achieve a better standard of life for himself.

Psychological factors will predominate where parents set a high premium on learning from an early age, and, by direct and indirect means communicate to the child the importance of learning, and of success in learning, as a criterion of self-evaluation. In some extreme cases love itself is made to appear conditional upon achievement.

The child gets the idea that love will be withheld unless he meets the learning demands imposed upon him, and which, in turn, can cause the major part of his own self-regard and esteem to be dependent upon what he achieves. Such people are to be found in most walks of life, and sad figures some of them are — being still firmly committed to a view of themselves which is positive only so long as they are out-stripping their peers. In this way they are unconsciously perpetuating the earlier assessment of their worth, bequeathed to them by their parents.

It may appear to some readers that what we are discussing here is really learning rather than intelligence. This is because the two are very closely linked. Some would even go so far as to say that intelligence is an amalgam of learned skills. But, for the purposes of this question and answer on operational intelligence, the important point I want to make is that in this matter of 'using his brains', or however we care to view it, the individual has a degree of choice in the matter of how much or how little he does, both in terms of developing his intelligence, and in putting it to use when he has acquired it.

One of the most potent motivating factors in all human behaviour is success. When children appear to lack motivation it does not mean that they would not like to succeed. In most cases, what happens initially is that they approach formal learning with a positive attitude and a desire to succeed but, when their experience or failure accumulates beyond a certain point they tend to opt out of the unequal struggle. It is really a measure of self-protection. Rather than be at continuing risk of experiencing further failure, they effectively avoid it by opting out.

Unfortunately this is often misconstrued as laziness by parents and teachers, and even more pressure is put on the child, usually with the opposite effect to what is intended.

Where parents sometimes go wrong is in exaggerating the degree of control a child has over his achievement in this regard. Too often they proceed on the basis that only a lack of effort stands between him and a much better level of performance.

I hope readers will be able to accept that in many cases this is not so. And in a significant number of these, it will not be because the child is dull.

How is intelligence affected by maturation? Is there really such a thing as a late-developer?

You will often hear people say of a child, 'he is not very mature for his age'. This can refer to his presentation in a physical sense — that is his size and general appearance — or to aspects of his behaviour, such as his emotional and intellectual development.

How should these impressions be viewed. Do they have any validity, or should they be avoided and ignored?

Though they are inevitably crude observations and certainly unscientific, there is a sense in which they have some basis in fact.

Because we find it convenient we tend to group children according to their chronological ages: they come into school at five, they leave at sixteen and so on. But because two children happen to be born on the same day, we should not assume that their development — especially their total or 'organismic' development — is going to proceed, step-by-step, at precisely the same pace and on all fronts. This clearly is not what happens.

In some cases there are known factors affecting a child's development from birth, or a very early age — such as illness for example.

On the other hand, there are also many other children whose development is slow for no apparent or identifiable reason. In other words, there is a discrepancy between their chronological ages and their developmental or organismic ages. Unfortunately, the demands of real life situations do not take any account of this, and we have to act for all practical purposes on the basis that development proceeds at a standard rate, and children of similar age are given similar educational opportunities. Not only this. In trying to establish what a child's general ability is, we have to take account of this one universal constant in the equation: that is, his chronological age. Not all intelligence tests use the concept of mental age, but no measure can avoid making reference to the child's chronological age at some point if it is to be of any value. In providing for his individual needs his performance has to be set against what is the norm, or standard for his age group, and what is being achieved by his peers.

There is currently a trend towards moving away from this unsatisfactory state of affairs towards a more realistic approach in making appropriate educational provision for the individual child's needs. The 1981 Act itself incorporates legislation which will promote this policy.

Basically, what truly equitable comprehensive education should do — as an ideal — is provide for the optimal intellectual and educational development of every individual child. I say as an ideal because, it is, of course, unattainable. At some point reference has to be made to his standing — both intellectually and in terms of his attainment — relative to that of others. However insightful and sensitive to the needs of the individual child provision might be, it cannot totally avoid this.

Nor would it be desirable in social and psychological terms, however effective it might be in promoting his progress in a narrow educational sense.

So far as practical circumstances allow some exclusively individual provision is already being made, specifically in the case of (some) slow-learning children, or where an individual child has a special need. In these situations, and for the purposes of achieving specific educational objectives, all reference to norms or standards can be set aside and the child's progress assessed purely in terms of his own best efforts and performance.

This involves the use of so-called criterion-referenced tasks which are closely related to his own ability in a particular area or subject, and without regard to what others of his own age or ability might be achieving. In these situations, all considerations of mental age, IQ or standard scores are irrelevant and are ignored.

Some people might feel that there is an obligation on education authorities to provide for the optimal intellectual and educational development of every child. This is not only impracticable, it is not in the best interests of children themselves. Physical, social and emotional aspects of childrens' needs have also to be provided for, and this can only be done within a school 'community'. If individual children are isolated in order to meet exceptional needs,

50

there is a point beyond which this becomes unacceptable and counter-productive.

A child may have strengths and potential for development quite independent of his cognitive abilities in a narrow sense, and it is right and certainly in his own best interests that they should be developed to the full. Some parents (and educators) are still setting too high a value on formal educational achievement in a narrow sense. As is said elsewhere in this book, it is the whole child that we should be concerned with, and with the promotion of his development on the broadest possible front.

With the character and the demands of society changing so rapidly it is becoming increasingly clear that educational achievement, (in a narrow sense), will count for less and less, in comparison with the development of social and other self-fulfilling skills. These latter are becoming more and more important in determining the quality of life for the individual.

If my child is not intelligent does it mean that he will not be able to achieve much educationally?

No. Many children, with IQs as low as 60 have acquired useful standards of literacy and numeracy. The important thing is that they must be efficient learners — at their level of general ability. If they are efficient learners, and have applied themselves well in the formal learning situation there is no reason why they should not perform to their mental age level. Thus a boy or girl who has only a modest level of ability, but who has been an efficient learner during their school careers, could be leaving at sixteen with attainments at the nine to ten year level. This would be a useful standard of attainment in both literacy and numeracy — certainly adequate to enable them to be gainfully employed in the community. The most important consideration here is that they should be conscientious and reliable workers.

Evidence shows that the intellectually less able often make highly reliable employees, giving good value for money in

51

terms of effort and work done, as well as finding satisfaction for themselves in their achievement.

HISTORICAL NOTE

What is the nature of intelligence?

Since it first clawed its way out of the primeval slime intelligence has, in a sense, been struggling towards an understanding of its own nature. It can be held that this is what evolution is about. Certainly one general definition of intelligence is expressed basically in these terms: that it is the individual's ability to adapt to its environment. The truth is that we are far from understanding fully most aspects of mental life and, although man has taken himself to the moon, has delved deep into his own unconscious motivations, and has contrived marvels of electronic modelling of some aspects of brain function through computer technology, he has, as yet, only the beginnings of an understanding of the processes which subserve human behaviour.

The main area of debate is concerned with the question of whether intelligence is primarily innate and therefore determined by biological and genetic factors, or whether it is primarily acquired, and determined by the individual's environment and life experiences.

One resolution of this problem was proposed by a neurologist, Hebb, who suggested calling the innate component Intelligence A, and the acquired component Intelligence B. The former, consisting as it does in the dimensions and quality of the individual's central nervous system could never be independently assessed, but could only be inferred from the quality of the individual's behaviour — as determined by experience and learning.

Assessment of the acquired component presents difficulties of its own, as we have seen, in that intelligent behaviour in the course of everyday living is not the same thing as intelligent behaviour in the structured situation of an IQ test. The one cannot be seen as directly implying or determining the other. A high IQ does not mean that an individual always can, and always will behave intelligently, in all situations.

Vernon, one of the most prolific workers in the field of the measurement of human abilities proposed a futher partial resolution of this dilemma by proposing yet another designation, Intelligence C, which refers to the product of the · individual's performance on an intelligence test. In other words his IQ. (His views are constantly being updated and a useful summary of his present position is contained in his paper to the Scottish Council for Research in Education, on the occasion of his being awarded a fellowship in 1978).

As mentioned earlier in this chapter one of the main supporters of the capacity theory — that intelligence is mainly determined by inheritance — was Sir Cyril Burt. Writing in 1975 he says:

'When two contributory factors, such as heredity and environment, interact with one another, the obvious procedure is to look for situations in which first one factor and then the other is relatively constant, and observe the result. During my work for the London County Council I had access to its orphanages and other residential institutions and to the confidential files of case-records summarising the family histories of the various inmates. My co-workers and I were thus able to study large numbers of children who had been transferred thither during the earliest weeks of infancy, and had been brought up in an environment that was practically the same for all. We found that individual differences in intelligence, so far from being diminished, varied over an unusually wide range. In the main they proved to be correlated with differences in the intelligence of one or both of the parents. The most striking instances were those of illegitimate children of high ability: often the father (so the case-records showed) had been a casual acquaintance of a social and intellectual status well above that of the mother, and had taken no further interest in the child. In such cases it is out of the question to ascribe the high intelligence of the child to the special cultural opportunities furnished by the environment, since his only home has been the institution. Similarly, when a child of dull parents happened to have been adopted in early infancy by a highly intelligent couple in the professional class, the intelligence of the child as he grew up almost invariably resembled the intelligence of his own parents rather than that of his foster parents. Thus in a society like our own it appears impossible to regard environmental differences as the dominant factor, so far as capacity is concerned.'

Any consideration of the concept of intelligence must include reference to the views of Piaget, the Swiss psychologist. His view is that the nature of functional intelligence changes as a child develops, and thus his perceptions of situations and problems, and his strategies for meeting them, progress in stages as he grows older.

The first of these he calls sensori-motor ability, which enables the child to come to terms with his physical environment — from birth to around two years of age. The period beyond this, to about seven years of age he denotes the pre-operational period, when the child reveals the characteristically naive logic of his age, interpreting the world as he sees it and not as he later discovers it to be.

This leads on, through a usually long transitional period of concrete operations when, as Piaget demonstrates with a wealth of example, children's conceptions of the world and how it works are remarkably universal, and seem to follow the same general progression — if at varying ages. Finally, this progresses to what he terms the formal intelligence of the adult.

The debate on the nature of intelligence will go on as long as we have to continue with our present meagre understanding of how physical and behavioural aspects of mental life are related. This is likely to be for some time. Meanwhile, I would argue that both the capacity view of intelligence, as mainly determined by the quality of the central nervous system and the environmentalist view, that it is mainly determined by the quality of the individual's environment and life experiences, both fail to take sufficient account of a third group of very specific factors which determine the efficiency of the individual's perceptual processes and, hence, his effective intelligence in certain formal learning situations.

A big question lies over the actual nature of this specificity. In what way, in neurological terms, can it be specific?

To be speculative, my own belief is that the work of the ethologists may point the way. We have known since the pioneer work of Tinbergen and others that a lot of animal behaviour, often apparently 'intelligent' in character, is, in fact, determined by distinct mechanisms, having highly specific functions. Could it be that some of our human skills — particularly our capacity to deal with symbolic material — are the result of genetic programming of this or a similar kind. That some of our perceptual abilities are not acquired as learned skills, but are largely, if not entirely, congenital and innate?

Certainly Tinbergen held the view that in some respects the cerebral cortex might be 'over-rated' and that elements of human behaviour could be essentially mechanistic, but are now heavily disguised through learning and acquired patterns of behaviour.

Of all the characteristics which mark us off from other life forms, including the primates, our use of language and our ability to symbolise it is the most profound. But for this one open sesame, this key to thought and communication, we should not find ourselves so elevated and remote from the rest of our fellow creatures.

The use of language is a comparatively recent acquisition and it is not surprising that our ability to use it, particularly in symbolised form, is peculiarly vulnerable to all kinds of adverse experience whether identifiable or not. For this reason evidence that some cases of specific learning disability appear to be genetic and inherited should not surprise us.

Again, evidence from the precocious infant reader and the child with Down's Syndrome who reads well, is easily reconcilable with this view. In this latter case, the innate 'programming' for this particular skill has not been affected by the otherwise massive genetic aberration.

Over recent years, there has been increasing attention given to the concept of creativity, arising mainly from the view that conventional intelligence tests have sometimes failed to identify individuals who clearly were capable of original and imaginative thought.

This idea which, with others, is only briefly mentioned here, is of particular interest in the context of this book, in the sense that the interest in creativity in some individual cases might well be associated with the fact that they have been handicapped through specific learning disabilities, and, thereby prevented from fulfilling themselves through traditional forms of educational achievement.

It could be that it has been for these reasons that some of them have turned to the arts and other modes of self-expression, and it is possible that this is more common than is realised, even by themselves.

Another very topical group of people deserve mention in this context. It has long been my view that many of the adult illiterates who are now receiving help within the Adult Literacy Scheme have among them some highly intelligent people — on any definition of that term. They are inclined to attribute their earlier failure to become literate to a variety of causes, including their own (obvious) dullness, indifference or lack of interest on the part of their parents, poor teaching or insufficient effort on their part. Plausible though this may sound, a more likely explanation is that these are the earlier generation of perceptually disabled individuals and no such blame for their failure attaches to themselves or others.

While many of them will continue to experience difficulty, their ability to approach the task of learning to read in a more objective and mature way offers a promise of success which they richly deserve — both for their courage and for the fact that they were, in any case, 'innocent' of what earlier charges were made against them.

Finally, there is that admirable band, sometimes referred to as self-made-men, who have made a success of their lives in a number of spheres, but who would make no claim to any significant degree of formal education; indeed, a number have been and are illiterate. There are good examples to be found in the farming community but, others have been equally successful in a variety of practical occupations — sometimes achieving managerial status or establishing their own companies.

The existence of these stalwarts must stand as an encouragement to young people who encounter severe difficulties in their formal learning and gives a special meaning to the old saying, 'He's got brains, he doesn't need education'.

SUMMARY

● For all practical purposes intelligence has to be viewed as a quality of behaviour. It has no meaning or existence except in behaviour.

● The important question is how educable is your child? For the teacher this becomes 'Can I teach this child?' A high IQ is of little value if it can't be translated into intelligent behaviour.

● Formal learning in the classroom — particularly in the early years — is dependent upon certain perceptual capacities. These allow the development of certain skills and these skills in turn are the prerequisites of certain types of learning.

● It is in dealing with symbolic or written information that these skills are most important. Some children can do a lot of things and show their intelligence in a number of ways but are unable to cope with the problem of reading.

● In the measurement of intelligence children are required to do a lot of different tasks. Success on some of these tasks is of greater significance for learning than success on others. But these strengths and weaknesses are not shown up in a simple statement of the IQ.

● It is the distribution and nature of these successes and failures that is important. Thus two children can obtain the same IQ but one will be a more efficient learner than the other.

● The IQ is a statistical concept. It is not an essential characteristic of the individual but an expression of his performance compared with the performance of others on a particular set of tasks.

● Intelligence and educability are seen to be different things. Some learning is dependent upon general reasoning ability but other types of learning – such as learning to read – are mainly dependent upon efficient perceptual skills. Reasoning ability will help, but it can't do the whole job. Intelligence can't work until information is available to it in an intelligible form.

● Because intelligence is a matter of behaviour it is affected by environmental factors. These influences are particularly important in the early years. Mental development is rapid during this period and the attention and stimulation a child receives at this time will have special significance for later years.

● Development is a natural process and extremes of intervention should be avoided. Whatever gain might be achieved in one area is likely to be at the cost of something equally important.

● Motivation will always be an important factor in achievement. Most children are highly motivated — if only because the desire to succeed is universal. When a child fails it is seldom because he is lazy. If he appears to be lazy the likelihood is that he is opting out of a situation where he is unable to meet the demands being made of him.

● It is important for a child to know that what he is able to achieve is not the only thing that determines what he is worth as an individual.

● Educational fulfilment should not be thought of in terms of narrow scholastic achievement. The development of other self-fulfilling skills are likely to be of increasing importance.

2

WHAT IS PERCEPTION?

Introduction

The subject of sensation has been exhaustively studied and we have a relatively full understanding of the sense organs, together with their anatomy, physiology and function. What we know very little about (and as yet only by inference), are the higher processes which give sensation 'meaning' and utility in our learning and mental life generally. This is perception.

In formal learning, that is the purposive learning which takes place in the classroom, there are two main channels of information — those of hearing and sight. Neither the eyes nor the ears work as a simple mechanical apparatus as, say, a camera or a microphone: they are infinitely complex organs. However, here we are concerned with the processes of perception which are, again, more complex than the function of the sense organs concerned. We say processes of perception because perception is not an instantaneous act and, like all processes it occupies time. And it is what happens during this process in both visual (seeing), and auditory (hearing), perception which has particular significance for learning.

When it comes to symbolic material, such as the written word, the complexity of the processes involved is such that there is little understanding or general agreement among neurologists and psychologists as to what actually occurs. What we do know is that the functioning of these processes is sometimes inefficient — due to an inadequacy or defect — with varying adverse consequences for the learning ability of the individual concerned.

Most of what has been written on this subject has been concerned with the interpretation of experimental results, (usually involving adults). Also, visual perception has come in for more attention than auditory perception which, for the understanding of the processes involved in formal learning, is unfortunate. We need to know more about the processes of auditory perception and the aspect of short-term memory in particular. It is at this level and beyond that our knowledge of brain function is conspicuously inadequate and, as yet we can only draw inferences from overt behaviour — including controlled experimentation — as to what is going on.

Looking at the individual human being, if we consider sensation at its lowest level there is probably little difference between the sensory experience of one person and another. Sensations of sound, light, smell, touch and taste. It is when we go beyond this point that individual factors determine perception and make it a qualitatively different experience from one individual to another, depending as it does on past experience on the one hand and the capacity of the individual brain and the efficiency of its perceptual processes on the other. However similar our sense organs might be in structure and in function, no two persons' perception will ever be the same.

The main objective of this chapter is to consider the implications of the fact that the capacity to deal with certain types of symbolic material — specifically the written word — appears to be distributed in the population without direct association with an individual's intelligence level.

The acquisition of any skill whether cognitive (mental) or physical (motor) for that matter — if not directly dependent upon intelligence, should certainly not be hindered by it. Logically, we would expect the intelligent child to acquire it at least as readily and to as high a degree as the less intelligent child. But this is not always the case. The evidence is that certain primary aspects of these processes may not be acquired through learning. This has to be considered in some detail and, at the outset it is essential to draw a distinction between the perceptual skills themselves — which by definition can be learned — and the neurological capacities upon which the learning of these skills depends.

The aspects of perception involved in perceiving and interpreting symbolic (written) material for instance — and which involve the unique capacity of short-term memory — appear to be more determined by constitutional factors and are not responsive to training in the way that learned skills are. Thus we should perhaps view this aspect of perception as a capacity rather than a skill, and should use the term short-term memory with caution, implying as it does that there is something going on which can be learned.

The recent usage of terms such as echoic memory (for short-term auditory memory), and iconic memory (for short-term visual memory) are helpful to some extent, in that they at least imply a qualitative difference between the retention of novel, symbolic material (as is involved in learning to read), and the retention or remembering of meaningful material or events.

We all know of children who are non-readers, some of whom may also be of low general ability, who can recall vividly experiences they have had and who are able to describe these experiences orally in a detailed way — sometimes demonstrating something approaching total recall. What they are doing is recounting an experience which they both understood and possibly enjoyed. Parents sometimes refer to a child's ability to do this and to his 'marvellous memory': which indeed he has for events and experiences of this kind. In these instances the brain is not being called upon to process and to organise raw, disconnected sense data. The experience hangs together as a whole. The sights and sounds and possibly other sensations were all immediately accessible and enjoyable to the child. And they were certainly meaningful. He understood what was happening, it was intelligible to him, and the whole experience could have been invested with joy, pleasure or excitement, all of which would help him to recall the experience at a later date.

In my early days of teaching I well remember an experience when I was working in a school for slow-learning pupils. This was in London in mainly pre-television days and the alternative attraction was the cinema. In the particular class I had responsibility for it had become established practice that, every Thursday afternoon, one (very popular) fifteen-year-old boy would recount his most recent cinema experience to the rest of the class. Despite his significantly low general ability he would proceed, with a complete absence of self-consciousness, to give a graphic account of the film (complete with sound effects – particularly the firing of pistols), holding his audience, including me, completely spellbound. He would be on his feet for hardly less than an hour, and there can't have been much in the way of the plot or even dialogue that was left out.

This is a perfect example of long-term memory and recall.

The use of oral language such as this is only a very small part of our communication system.

In learning to read a child has to make sense of new and essentially meaningless material.

For about six thousand years now (which isn't very long in evolutionary terms), we have been recording our experience and communicating with each other and with succeeding generations through the use of symbols. Symbols or signs which stand for or represent our thoughts and ideas. (It can be small comfort to anyone but, had this not happened there would certainly be no such concept or problem as dyslexia).

Using symbols and acquiring a facility for interpreting them makes new and very different demands on our brains and perceptual apparatus. And, as we all know, a great deal of the factual information children have to absorb in the course of their formal learning is only to be found in books in this form. There is no way that they can extract this information except by cracking the code — or acquiring the decoding skill, as reading is sometimes described.

So what about these perceptual processes involved in the interpretation of symbolised information. Are they skills and therefore accessible to training? Or are they capacities. Something 'given' which must exist before the appropriate skill can be developed?

If they are skills it would mean that an efficient teacher, not necessarily a specialist teacher — or a parent for that matter — could take a child through a course of training, using material designed to exercise a particular capacity to process sensory information, (auditory or visual according to need), and, by doing so improve his efficiency as a learner. Unfortunately, what accumulated experience seems to show is that children with severe deficiencies in these capacities are not capable of making them good through concentration on the areas of weakness themselves, but, on the contrary, appear to need to find alternative routes to perceptual competence — which may well involve quite different strategies from those employed by normal or non-disabled children.

The capacities themselves do not appear to be affected by training — as say a muscle can be made stronger through exercise — but tend to remain imperfect throughout the individual's life. Some highly intelligent adults with this problem who, through various strategies have acquired a useful standard of literacy, nevertheless retain the same, and apparently enduring disability: as demonstrated in their inability to cope with certain tasks — particularly such things as remembering telephone numbers, as well as new or unfamiliar words.

We should therefore think of these prerequisites to efficient reading as capacities to acquire skills, rather than skills in themselves. The term skill implies learning and, if the capacity to acquire it is not available, or is severely limited, the question of its accessibility to training has to be seen as limited as well. And, it will either not be acquired or, at best, be acquired with varying degrees of difficulty.

Logically the case for thinking that there should be some means of training these 'skills' is so strong that there is a danger of making unwarranted assumptions about how they are acquired, particularly as between one individual and another. The acquisition or learning of any cognitive skill does, by its nature, involve complex neurological organisation and function -- possibly with significant individual variation -- even when their development follows an apparently normal course. In cases where difficulty is encountered it is wrong to come to hasty conclusions as to what might be happening, particulary about the reasons for failure in any individual case. Or to assume, when they are surmounted, that this process invariably follows a similar course, with the implication that following it in other cases offers some guarantee of success.

It cannot be too strongly emphasised that when children apparently overcome the affects of perceptual deficits it is not the case that some major neurological change has been effected. It is simply that they have acquired these skills in different ways -- or indeed may be using different skills to achieve the same ends. However well they may compensate for these defects or anomalies, the chances are, that, in organic or physiological terms, the deficits still remain.

What remedial teachers (or others, including parents), are doing when they are helping a perceptually disabled child to read, is not 'undoing' or correcting some neurological condition, but helping the child to acquire essentially new and possibly different skills, often in quite unorthodox ways. Whatever works goes.

It is tenable, in this age of the computer, to view the brain in mechanistic terms and to see it as a highly developed, highly sophisticated instrument for processing information, and organising it in such a way that behaviour appropriate to any given situation results.

Continuing this mechanistic analogy; given an efficient machine, it will deal with the sensory input — with the information coming in — efficiently, it will deal with it in a relatively short space of time, and, it will produce the appropriate responses. If, on the other hand, wires are crossed, or there is a piece missing, or, (as I prefer to think is often the case) there is a biochemical deficiency or abnormality of some kind, then it will require more information to be fed into it in order to come up eventually with the appropriate response or, it will make an inappropriate response or, if the defects are sufficiently severe it will not respond at all.

This is a valid analogue or model for considering processes in the adult brain, but it does not hold when considering the immature, developing brain of the child.

A lot of our knowledge of brain function has come to us piecemeal and by accident — even literally. Some of the most significant pioneer work in this area was done during the first world war when Head and others were working with soldiers and other servicemen who had sustained brain injuries. His main work was on the phenomenon of aphasia — the loss of speech in such patients. Such a loss of function is what marks off, in a fundamental way the difference between an adult, mature brain, and the brain of a child. When some lesion occurs in an adult brain it results in a loss of function: something that previously was there is now no longer there. Whether it is a loss of speech or the use of a limb, the one universal characteristic is this loss of function. It is, of course, paralleled by the phenomena of senility — the dying off of brain cells in old age — when our faculties and skills desert us in a decisive and irreversible way.

Such conditions, resulting in a loss of function in adults, are described clinically by use of the negative prefix a - : aphasia (inability to produce speech), apraxia (inability

66

to manipulate objects), etc. On the other hand, where children are concerned, it is wrong to think in terms of a loss of function – which may not yet have been acquired – or may be only partially acquired. In such cases any abnormality occuring early in the course of a child's development will cause aspects of behaviour to be delayed and it is therefore more logical and intelligible to think in terms of a dysfunction rather than a loss of function. Here the prefix dys (Greek = bad) is used, as in the case of the celebrated if unfortunate dyslexia. This is also the reason why more recent definitions of this condition have been modified to include the word 'developmental' to distinguish it from disabilities acquired in later life.

The connection or association between the organic factor and the behavioural aspect must be extremely complex and subtle, because anomalies and apparent contradictions are found to co-exist on the most cursory examination. There are, for instance, the cases of known brain damage resulting in varying degrees of cerebral palsy or spasticity without any associated impairment of intellectual function. Many such people follow successful professional or otherwise intellectually demanding careers. In these cases the damage their central nervous systems have sustained has apparently been confined to the areas of the brain concerned with motor behaviour (movement), and has not affected the delicate and complex processes involved in the processing of symbolic material required in reading.

On the other hand, what is equally dramatic and anomalous is the existence of these perceptual disabilities in children who have no known significant medical history of any kind. This is one of the reasons why it is essential to think of these subtle neurological (or biochemical) defects in functional terms, rather than in terms of lesions or physical damage. Also, there is the evidence that in some cases the disability is inherited and also sex-linked, because there is known to be a higher incidence in boys than in girls.

There is a natural antipathy towards thinking of these

conditions as associated with brain damage, even the so-called 'minimal brain damage' or MBD which was in common usage for some time and is discussed later. Apart from its being a strongly emotive term, and a positive prescription for causing parents anxiety and distress, it implies a condition which may have no existence in fact.

The structure of the brain is so complex that there should be no difficulty in conceiving of a disorder or defect in its function – especially when, in evolutionary terms, only recently acquired skills such as those involved in dealing with symbolic material are concerned – without, at the same time, having to visualise some associated physical or structural pathology.

A more reasonable view to take would be that in such a complex organ as the brain, minor biochemical or electrical aberrations in its function – possibly associated with the absence or deficiency of an enzyme or neuro-transmitter yet to be discovered – can have significant behavioural effects. A failure to deal efficiently with symbolic, particularly written information, would appear to be one of these.

Although it is primarily when we are confronted with learning failure in the intelligent child that we really sit up and take notice we should not run away with the idea that defects in the processing of sensory information of this kind cannot occur in less able children. Because the general picture is obscured by their backwardness we are inclined not to pursue the more specific aspects of their learning problems but, as was said earlier, if they do have a constitutional basis, it is logical to assume that they will occur across the whole range of intellectual ability. Dyslexia, as defined, excludes the dull child, and this, in my view, is one of the causes of the confusion which has accumulated around this concept.

As we have seen, the two main channels of information in the formal learning situation are hearing and sight. Both are normally involved in the task of learning to read and it is of academic interest which of them is the more important, bearing in mind that it is not the sense data themselves but the way they are processed in the brain that is of significance. If this were not the case, the apparent anomaly of the very dull child who reads well mechanically would be of no interest. Their hearing and vision is often acute. Also the blind and profoundly deaf frequently acquire this skill — the significance of which is also discussed later.

Our procedures for assessing these perceptual capacities are crude at present. In time, hopefully, we shall be better able to identify them and their function, as well as assess their efficiency and significance for learning. In the meantime, it is clear that learning difficulties are encountered — especially in the acquisition of the basic skills of mechanical reading and, to a lesser degree of arithmetic computation — in direct association with defects or deficiencies in these perceptual systems.

How can perceptual abilities be assessed?

Tests to assess perceptual skills relevant to the acquisition of reading — specifically 'decoding' or mechanical reading — must refer, on the one hand to an ability to organise and identify visual and auditory sensations and, on the other to an ability to 'hold' these sensations long enough for them to be linked together by association.*

Visually, simple copying tasks therefore are not adequate to establish this capacity. This can only be done by requiring the child to memorise what he sees for a limited time.

It goes without saying that what is to be reproduced in this way must be entirely novel and not something the child is familiar with.

Auditorily the same applies. In this case there is a need to establish a capacity for holding auditory configurations (sound shapes), long enough for the link or association to be made. There appears to be no better material for this assessment than the repetition of digits — and these are, of course easily randomised.

*See footnote at end of chapter.

How is visual perception assessed?

When a young child — say the average six or seven year old — has to copy a diamond shape he does not perceive it 'as a whole' and proceed to draw it 'as a whole'. He draws each of the four sides, one at a time, checking his lines as he goes along — often exaggerating the angles (although he has no concept of an angle at this stage) because although he sees the change in direction of line, he can only cope with them as he perceives them — that is as separate and individual parts. Later, when his ability to hold such a configuration in his head is adequate, he will perceive and draw it as a whole. To observe this typical 'immature' perception is often interesting. It is clear that the child 'sees' the angles — and he is determined to include them in his reproduction — with sometimes amusing results. See Fig. 1.

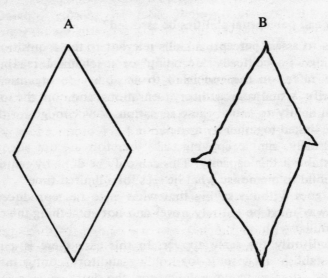

Fig. 1
This performance does not represent a standard or degree of skill but typifies a stage of development in perception. Note the exaggerated angles which indicate that the child has observed the change in direction of line (i.e. the angles,

though he has no concept of an angle at this stage), and has made sure of including them in his reproduction. He is not yet perceiving the diamond shape as a whole, but piecemeal. His effort should not be viewed as indicating defective, but immature perception.

At this stage it is too early to pick up the child who might be perceptually disabled in the sense we are concerned with because what he is engaged in is essentially a copying task. Totally different demands are made on the child's perceptual abilities when he has to reproduce something from memory.

If he is shown a relatively simple design and is given the opportunity of looking at it for a limited time (say) ten seconds, with the instruction . . . "Look at this carefully and try to remember it, because I am going to ask you to draw it afterwards", he has to draw on a perceptual capacity of a qualitatively different order. His sensory apparatus — his vision — however acute, is not going to see him through here. He not only has to see the design, he has to perceive it. This is the fundamental distinction between these two tasks. The one demanding only adequate vision and a simple executive ability to draw, the other demanding a capacity for processing and organising the visual information in such a way as will allow him to retain it and reproduce it at will.

Perceiving (visually) — the critical aspect

On the following pages are examples of two children's performances on a perceptual task.

The figure on the left (A) was shown to them for ten seconds with the instruction, "Look at this carefully and try to remember it, because I am going to ask you to draw it afterwards". The figure on the right (B) is what the child produced.

The results should not be viewed as standard performances or as representing degrees of disability. They are reproduced to show how these capacities vary between one

71

individual and another, and, more significantly, do not appear to be associated with the child's intelligence level. The intelligent child does not invariably produce the better design nor the dull child invariably the inferior one. The ability is clearly specific and the product of a distinct and separate capacity.

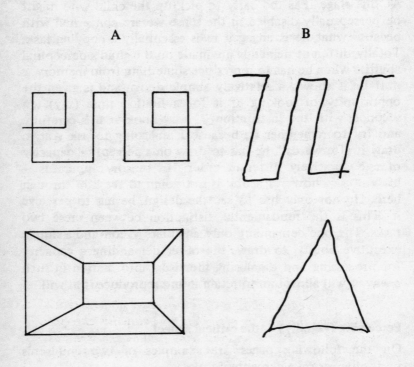

Fig. 2
Boy: Age 9 years 8 months.
Reading Age 7 years 10 months. (IQ = 143)
This highly intelligent boy (IQ = 143) was nearly ten years of age and reading at below the eight year level. His reproduction of designs shows a massively impaired visual perception.

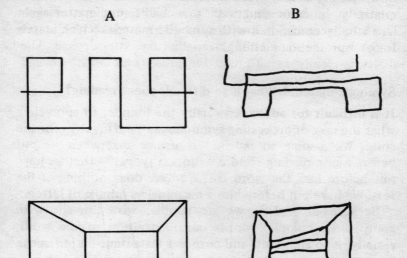

Fig. 3

Boy: Age 11/0 years.
Reading Age: 7 years 3 months. (IQ = 88)
This eleven-year-old boy is of low-average ability with a
reading-age three years nine months below his chrono-
logical age. His reproduction of the first design is almost
bizarre, the second is well below the expected level.

An interesting feature of this test is that though the time
element is critical in the case of some children, there
are others — in whom the disability is severe — who continue
to reproduce unacceptable and sometimes bizarre results
after prolonged or repeated presentations.

It is fascinating — in a purely academic sense — that
such a capacity apparently exists independently of intelligence

73

or reasoning ability. And here the child is dealing with a relatively concrete situation: it is a different matter again when he is confronted with symbolic material which stands for or represents something.

Symbolic material. What is so difficult about reading?

It is difficult for adults, especially the literate, to appreciate what the task of processing symbolic material involves for the child. We assume so much. We assume that when we put before a non-reading child a word — say, cat — that we have put before him the word cat. We have done nothing of the sort. We have put before him a meaningless jumble of letters.

Because, as readers, we are familiar with this and with many more complex words our recognition of the word, visually, is to all intents and purposes instantaneous but, more importantly, there is also instantaneous association between this symbol and its sound.

(The situation of children suffering from severe deafness is interesting in this context and is considered in detail in a case history.)

For a child with a specific learning disability the breakdown or dysfunction in this process may come at any point. Firstly, and this is relatively common, he may have difficulty in organising the visual input itself. The simplest visual configuration may not be represented in his brain in anything like the form we assume it is.

We know this because when we give children simple patterns to reproduce by manipulating blocks, or in other ways, they have difficulty in organising visual input of this kind at a quite elementary level. But a written symbol is not in any case a concrete object that you can pick up and manipulate. A symbol, by definition, is there to represent something: the child has to learn to make use of it as it is. Thus the visual image, whether it be a word or a single letter has to be held in the brain in such a way that whenever it occurs again it will be recognised. In the competent reader

74

instantaneously: in the less accomplished reader it will take longer. He needs more sensory input.

It is at this point that in a significant number of cases the breakdown occurs. The child with a specific reading disability of this type may be able to see things clearly enough: also to copy them, but he is unable to retain them long enough for them to be of any use in the learning process. It is at this advanced level of visual perception that the functional defects often occur.

The picture is complicated for some parents because they know that their child has been capable of 'remembering' what he sees — even from an early age. They, quite understandably, do not distinguish between short-term and long-term memory. To them a child is capable of remembering what he sees or he isn't: it's as simple as that.

Many times I have had recounted to me by parents instances of how their child has remembered details of a journey. Young children seem to be particularly receptive to experiences of this kind and notice all sorts of features and points of interest which are overlooked and not registered by adults. When, on a later occasion the child demonstrates his ability to recall these events with such detail and clarity it is not surprising that parents have difficulty in accepting that the child has a problem of short-term recall. The explanation, as was described earlier, lies in the fact that the child's brain is processing and organising totally different kinds of information.

How is auditory perception assessed?

The auditory equivalent of the visual process just described is in many ways more complex and, at the same time, apparently more important in the learning situation — particularly for reading.

In this case auditory configurations or 'sound shapes' as distinct from visual ones have to be processed and organised — in apparently much the same way — so as to allow the child to retain them usefully and to recall them at will.

Once again, this capacity can only be assessed with the use of meaningless material. We are not concerned with the child's hearing acuity (any more than we were concerned with his visual acuity), nor with his ability to remember meaningful information – such as a story or an interesting bit of news – but with his capacity for processing and organising new and unconnected bits of information.

If a child is asked to repeat a number of digits (single numbers) presented orally, at one second intervals, it will be found that the majority of seven-year-olds will repeat five digits accurately and repeatedly which is the norm for this age group – (six digits being the norm at the ten year level). Others will show obvious and sometimes dramatic failure in this task, managing perhaps only three digits reliably. In some cases these will be children of well over seven years of age, as well as some teenagers and adults.

Once again, it should be stressed that an important feature of this very specific ability is that it is not a function of general intelligence. Many children of low general ability are able to repeat digits in this way successfully, and many children of high general ability are not able to do it.

This part of the perceptual process is the auditory equivalent of the visual short-term memory discussed earlier. Here the sound or sound image has to be held in a form and for long enough to allow its association with other sense data: in reading, as we have seen, this would be the visual symbol of the word.

Say to a child – any child from seven years upwards:
"I want you to say these numbers after me: listen carefully: wait until I've finished, then you say them."

(one second intervals)

2 – 9 – 7 – 6 – 4
1 – 3 – 5 – 8 – 2
3 – 2 – 7 – 5 – 9

Repeating such a series accurately (once or more) is the norm for a seven-year-old.

If the child succeeds with five digits there is no reason why you should not proceed to present him with six:

$$9 - 5 - 8 - 3 - 6 - 1$$
$$8 - 4 - 2 - 7 - 9 - 6$$
$$5 - 2 - 3 - 8 - 1 - 9$$

This is the norm for the ten-year-old. But if an older child succeeds in doing it repeatedly and with ease, it is an indicator that there is nothing seriously wrong with his auditory perception.

Children will often indicate that they are having difficulty with this task through a puzzled frown, and then will proceed to reverse the last two digits or sometimes introduce one (or more) that has not been given.

It is not uncommon to observe in the older, intelligent child, signs of genuine distress at his failure to do something which he feels should be well within his capabilities. With such children it is good practice for psychologists or others to discuss this experience with them, emphasising that what they are having trouble with has nothing to do with their general intelligence, but is a very specific disability. In my professional work I have found it productive to discuss with some children how this particular failure has relevance for their learning difficulty. Many such children have found reassurance and new hope in hearing something explicit, explained in terms they can understand and which they can see has relevance for their own situation.

A number of researchers have discovered that the ability to succeed in this test does not correlate with — that is, does not appear to be related to — success on other tests. In other words that it is a highly specific ability. It is remarkable that some of these writers have not seen the possible significance of this in their results or, when they have, have not realised their significance for learning.

Psychologists generally, some involved in research as well as many in the educational field are beginning to recognise that this aspect of perception has a peculiar association with, and significance for the child's ability to process written material and, in consequence, for his ability to read.

In many cases of reading failure the problem seems to occur at this point in the perceptual process. It is not that the child does not hear sound, they can usually demonstrate acute hearing for simple sounds — say one to three digits — by repeating them accurately and consistently. They fail only when the demand on their auditory (echoic) memory exceeds this — as when they are asked to repeat five or more digits. It seems that this is a critical point in this highly specific perceptual capacity, and that a minimal requirement for learning to read mechanically is the ability to process auditory data of this complexity — particularly in the case of the younger child. But a note of caution here. It is possible that a perceptually disabled child who would not have succeeded in repeating the requisite numbers of digits at an earlier, critical age, does eventually acquire (with difficulty) the ability to do it. This does not mean that any problem which he might have had has gone away. He almost certainly has the relatively inefficient perceptual capacities he had earlier. The existence of adults who continue to have extreme difficulty with remembering telephone numbers would argue that the fundamental condition often remains unchanged although, by various strategies they, (and particularly the intelligent), will have found a variety of ways of coping with the problem and will have acquired varying degrees of literacy.

*Footnote — For readers who are professionally involved — the Stanford-Binet is a good example. When this excellent test was first devised the significance of some of the sub-tests was not recognised. (See the discussion of scatter in the chapter on Intelligence). In particular this is true of the Reproduction of Designs from Memory and the Repetition of Digits tests as indicators of perceptual deficits. The fact that evidence of the significance of these skills for formal learning is, belatedly becoming apparent — plus the fact that there are now a number of perceptual tests available — does nothing to detract from their essential relevance and suitability.

Implicit in these two tasks are, and always have been, all the essential elements for determining efficiency in the two major perceptual systems. Increasingly refined methods of assessing these aspects of mental ability are being devised, but it seems to me unlikely that any departure from the essential nature of these tests will produce dramatically new and/or more useful information. Hopefully, what they will do is help us to quantify and measure what is, by any standards, an extremely elusive quality.

SUMMARY

- Remembering, that is the storing in long-term memory of such things as stories, films or real-life experiences is something different from the short-term recording of new and unfamiliar information required for perception.

- It is this short-term recording that is defective in children who have this type of learning disability, not their ability to remember meaningful material and events.

- Evidence suggests that these processes are dependent upon the presence of certain innate or constitutional capacities within the individual — that is of a given rather than an acquired nature. They are capacities to acquire skills rather than skills in themselves.

- They do not appear to be responsive to training.

- In cases where these capacities are severely limited individuals need to find new and different routes to perceptual competence. How this is achieved is very much an individual process, depending on the child's general intelligence and his own peculiar strengths and weaknesses.

- The assessment of visual perception was illustrated and attention drawn to the difference between copying a figure and reproducing one from memory. Copying allows the individual to draw one bit at a time: reprodu-

79

cing something from memory demands that it is perceived as a whole.

● Attention was drawn to the special nature and difficulty of perceiving the written word. It is initially a meaningless shape and some children have difficulty in containing this meaningless shape in their heads long enough for it to be of any use in learning.

● In reading this use is the association of that shape with a sound: and for some children it is the sound that they are unable to contain accurately and for long enough for an association to be made.

● The fact that some of them hear and perceive sound perfectly within the compass of their short-term memory is demonstrated in their ability to repeat three digits. (Few fail to do this). It is beyond this point that the mischief occurs.

3

WHAT IS LEARNING?

A great deal has been written on the subject of learning, and it has always been one of the most important areas of study in academic and experimental psychology.

Appendix II at the end of the book discusses some current views of learning in a theoretical way which professional readers might find of interest and value.* Meanwhile, more practical aspects of formal learning are considered with particular reference to the perceptually disabled child.

There can be efficient learning at different levels. Often the levels exist independently of one another and can exist in different children.

Some children appear to have efficient perceptual processes and a facility for what might be termed low-level, associative learning, and give the impression of early promise but are unable to achieve a relative performance in later years. Gradually this rote learning has to progress to abstract and higher-order learning through understanding.

Conversely, there are children who, possessing inadequate or defective perceptual skills, put up a poor performance in the early years, but who come into their own eventually, and demonstrate a high level of learning ability when educational demands are qualitatively different and require comprehension and reasoning power of a different order.

The problem for the child with a specific learning disability

*It is inevitably somewhat technical and contains terms and language probably unfamiliar to the general reader.

is that if his disability is severe and illiteracy effectively isolates him from this area of learning for too long, it can mean that he does not achieve access to higher education — at least, not in the short-term.

Efficient assimilation and processing (perception) of information, in whatever form, is an essential prerequisite of learning. It is also clear that in formal learning most of this information is in symbolic (written) form, and requires to be decoded before it can be regarded as available to the child. Incidental, or informal learning, while being an essential element of all-round education, is not sufficient to allow the child to cope with the demands of the classroom nor to pass examinations, although many who do not acquire a high standard of literacy do go on to demonstrate great ability in practical and artistic pursuits.

A few exceptional individuals, with substantial learning disabilities, have blasted their way through to success in professional careers, and one notable example is included in the case histories. The commercial world too, and particularly the farming community can boast a number of eminently successful men who would not lay claim to any degree of 'book-learning'.

Why do some children learn well in the early years and not so well later?

The importance of the specificity of certain skills, as opposed to an all-round general ability, (the 'g' factor), particularly for early learning, has not been sufficiently recognised. Some children, because they have good perceptual skills, are efficient early learners, and can cope with most of the demands of the primary and early junior years impressively. If, on the other hand, they do not have good general intelligence and reasoning ability, their early promise will fall off. This accounts for the relatively late discovery of some children of very modest ability, who are referred to specialist agencies for the first time as teenagers because they are presenting behaviour problems. This is not to say that they should have been removed to different learning environments, but it does mean that we should be alert to the danger of assuming too much about children's general ability on the basis of their early performance, particularly in reading. There is an understandable, and sometimes irresistible tendency in teachers to equate early reading with intelligence. (After all, apart from the child's general presentation, it is the only objective measure of his ability immediately available in the classroom). Among other things, it can lead to unrealistic expectations on the part of parents and teachers, who might understandably expect such children to fulfil their early promise and to achieve good standards of attainment throughout their school careers.

One infallible clue to identifying early readers of this type — that is those of modest general ability — is the quality of their comprehension and understanding of what they have read. Teachers, and particularly parents, should be on their guard against assuming that if a child is able to read a passage fluently, he should, per se, be able to understand it.

One of the frustrating experiences for teachers in these situations is that of being confronted by those who certainly could understand — if they could read — alongside those who can read with ease but fail to understand.

Unfortunately this sort of understanding or comprehension can not be taught. This is operational intelligence in its essence. (It has been my view for many years that if we were to be restricted to one, and only one test of an individual child's educability, the task of summarising and extracting meaning from a passage of prose would be the most valid and reliable.)

I have also come across a number of pupils who demonstrate the effectiveness of good perceptual systems and rote memory at a higher level. They are to be found among boys and girls of average ability who, in some cases, are not imaginative or capable of very original thought. However, with some effort — often only towards the end of their

'O' level courses — they achieve results which surprise their peers, their teachers, and even their parents, not to mention themselves.

In subjects which do not demand the understanding of rules — English Literature as opposed to English Language, (grammar), for instance — they are capable of absorbing impressive amounts of factual information which they duly reproduce at examination time. This again distinguishes one type of learning from another, or one level from another: the two being well represented in the Ordinary Level and Advanced Level of the General Certificate of Education.

At some point the individual student has to bring a critical faculty to bear upon what he knows as opposed merely to reproducing it, and this is what separates the student who is successful at 'A' level and who could realistically go on to Higher Education and a degree course, from the student who has an impressive rote learning capacity and memory, but who lacks the insight and imaginative intelligence which the majority of academic courses demand. On the other hand, such students could be eminently suited for some advanced technical courses, where an ability to absorb large amounts of information is the main attribute required.

One of the less happy consequences of being an efficient learner, up to the GCE 'O' level standard, is that some students who are open-minded about their own careers, find themselves under pressure when they have produced an impressive crop of 'O' level results. To many teachers and parents the child's ability to do this is argument enough that he or she must proceed to higher education, (usually a degree course), or be deemed to be throwing away their opportunities and wasting their lives.

Some of the more perceptive among these young people know that what they have achieved they have achieved through rote learning and that they are not suited to the demands of higher academic courses. Some, unfortunately, are persuaded to take a different view and find themselves in a university, frequently to the astonishment of their tutors, when they would be much better suited to, and certainly would be happier in intellectually less demanding situations.

What about the intelligent child with a learning disability?

Older children who are perceptually disabled but otherwise of good general ability tend to compensate for this loss by developing their capacity to learn from what they hear. They are generally motivated and apply themselves with a high level of concentration in learning situations where they are not disadvantaged. These would include all oral lessons, all lessons where visual and sound aids are used, as well as a whole range of observational studies. Their main handicap is their inability to take down legible notes but, even here, the increasing use of tape-recorders is making this less severe − particularly where more advanced study is concerned.

Of course nothing can fully compensate the poor reader for his inability to get information from books. But, given sufficient motivation − which the intelligent child has if his situation is well managed − a great deal of short-fall can be made up. The cost, mainly, will be in terms of time. He will take longer to achieve comparable educational objectives relative to his non-disabled peers.

Do social factors play a part in learning?

Children with substantial and specific learning disabilities come from all social classes. The idea that if a child has come from a poor background his problem must be due to his background is to risk doing him a grave disservice and to risk overlooking his true educational needs. Certainly, as a minimum provision in a civilised society his social and material situation should be made good where possible, but we should not be beguiled into thinking that this is going to cause his learning problem to disappear. The social inequalities which undoubtedly exist have no logical bearing

85

on these kinds of disabilities.

Evidence is accumulating, particularly since the Plowden Report, that social factors must be held to be partly responsible for the poor educational progress of some children, especially in the early years. Lack of general care and provision, and a paucity of stimulation and language experience in the home being particularly relevant in this context.

However, the disabilities which are the subject matter of this book are, by definition, of constitutional origin, and have nothing to do with poor environmental conditions, inadequate parenting, malnutrition or lack of material provision of any kind. They are to be found in children from all social classes. Obviously, any problem a child has, whether it is primarily educational, emotional or social, will be exacerbated by poor environmental conditions, and, certainly the child with a specific learning disability is going to be doubly disadvantaged if he is handicapped through his living conditions as well. While recognising that some children's lack of progress can be directly associated with emotional and social factors these cases are, in my view, far out-numbered by those which have their origin in inadequate or defective perceptual skills.

One of the main problems in this area is that, due to the emotive aspect, (of regarding these disabilities as having a constitutional basis), it is assumed that all such disabilities must, inevitably, be severe. There is no reason why this view should be taken, nor that they should all be regarded as equally intractable and resistant to remedial teaching. Many of them are extremely slight — though none-the-less specific for this — and this is what causes them to be viewed as essentially developmental, rather than implying any permanent disability. The most severe on the other hand do appear to be enduring — as we have seen, in some cases into adult life. It is, as with many other conditions, a question of degree rather than of a difference in their essential nature.

If mechanical reading is a low-grade skill, what prevents the intelligent child from acquiring it?

When the term low-grade is used it must be seen as referring to the total hierarchy of neurological capacities which determine cognitive development. Whatever the neurological basis of this skill is, it must be significant that it can be acquired by less able children: also, that, in the young precocious reader, (there are many four-year-olds who read), it appears just to happen, without intensive effort on the child's part, nor, more significantly on the part of anyone else. These cases argue that there is an essentially mechanical process operating — including efficient perceptual processing — rather than higher-order intellectual processes, or reasoning ability. It is in this sense that there is some justification in referring to it as a low-grade skill.

The functional intelligence or reasoning ability of the four-year-old is not, at this stage of his development, likely to be the significant factor.*

Learning disabled children cannot be protected from early failure. The aim must be to minimise their experience of failure and to place them in a learning environment which does not cause them to be seen — or to see themselves — as different in some fundamental way: and where all their other capacities and learning skills can be exploited to the full.

We cannot really have it both ways: that is avoid singling them out and treating them differently on the one hand, and, at the same time put them into special learning environments outside the mainstream of education on the other.

No child who is considered to have a specific learning disability should be excused on the grounds that there are

*I have made the point earlier that this evidence suggests that there may be a specific innate factor (possibly in the nature of genetic programming) operative here. The view is frankly speculative; but I make no apology for including it. Hopefully it will stimulate others to pursue what I believe will be a fruitful line of enquiry.

good reasons for his failure, and he can, therefore, be allowed to slack. On the contrary, he has to get the message early that he has to work harder than others to keep up or even to move at a reasonable pace. It is not a let-out and should never be viewed as such.

Some parents of these children appear to behave as though achieving an admission that their child is learning-disabled is a solution in itself. But at best this is only the beginning of what could be a long, hard haul for the child and his teachers. If his disability is severe, there is no way that he is going to achieve significant improvement in his formal attainments, except through hard graft.

The greatest contribution his parents can make is to accept this themselves and to support him in the process of accepting it himself. He will need their understanding and encouragement in order to cope with the frustrations he will experience, and to meet the extra demands which will be made of him.

To think that some agency can take over and do the work is a fantasy. It has to be done by the child. He needs help — and should get it. But no one can do his learning for him.

SUMMARY

● Some children make impressive early progress — particularly in reading — because they are capable of efficient visual and auditory perception. They will not all be highly intelligent and some will be of only modest ability.

● It is a mistake to equate early reading with good general ability. Not all of these children will be able to perform equally well later or in other areas of learning.

● Teachers and parents should guard against assuming that a child who reads well will necessarily understand all that he reads. How much he understands will be determined by other factors, including his general intelligence.

● Some pupils have efficient perception, are good at rote learning and remember well. They are good achievers up to a certain level — where accumulating factual information is important.

● Older pupils who have a specific learning disability (and are therefore poor readers) generally make good use of their hearing in the classroom. The more able ones who wish to proceed to higher education can be helped through the use of teaching aids.

● Social factors, while always relevant to a child's performance have no direct bearing on specific learning disabilities of this kind. They occur in all classes of society.

● The question of mechanical reading as a low-grade skill was discussed. The evidence that something in the nature of genetic programming is operating is strong. The skill is unlikely to be dependant upon reasoning ability in the case of the less able child nor in that of the precocious four-year-old.

4

WHAT IS MINIMAL BRAIN DAMAGE?

Introduction

To take a child who shows evidence of a severe learning
problem to a neurologist for a full investigation may appear
to be a sound idea, and many parents who are concerned
about their child's situation will press for this. However,
they should not be surprised if the neurologist gives him a
clean bill of health and the reassuring information that he
can find no abnormality.

Neurologists are concerned to establish whether or not
there are any abnormalities of the nervous system, (particularly of the central nervous system, comprised of the brain
and spinal chord), which can be adversely affecting normal
behaviour in a fairly narrow, clinical sense. They are concerned to discover whether there are any so called hard signs
of neurological malfunction and, generally speaking, are not
disposed to recognise subtle signs of learning disabilities as
coming within their province. Thus it can be a frustrating
experience – albeit a basically reassuring one – for a parent
in this situation to be told that there is nothing wrong.

It comes back to the vexing problem of disagreement
between different specialists – and sometimes between
individuals within the same specialism – as to whether
or not there is a case to be made for concluding that some
children's learning problems might be associated with
constitutional factors.

Nothing has so bedevilled attempts to deal with the

problem of constitutionally based learning disabilities as the idea of brain damage. The purpose of this chapter is to stress the importance of conceiving of such disabilities as essentially functional in nature, rather than being preoccupied with trying to identify the underlying pathology itself.

It should be understood that, in all cases, we are concerned with very early events or conditions in the course of the child's development, and not with damage sustained through disease or accident in later years. Although physical, including neurological development, proceeds into teenage or later, it is the period of early development which is critical for the subject matter of this chapter. It has to be seen as largely confined to the period of pregnancy, through birth and the perinatal period.

The reason for this distinction, as mentioned earlier, is that the effects on the infant's developing central nervous system, when the actual processes of neurological growth and organisation are beginning to take place, are both qualitatively and quantitatively different from the effects of damage sustained during later stages of development, or when, for all practical considerations, such development can be said to have taken place.

Obviously major events during childhood, particularly during the formative years – nought to five or six – will have their relative importance, but no period has quite the degree of significance as these early days.

Gross brain damage

Before considering the difficult concept of minimal brain damage, it would be helpful to take a look at the better understood area of gross brain damage and its consequences.

There are many different kinds and causes of this, some associated with physiological factors, such as severe toxaemia during a critical period of pregnancy; others associated with particularly difficult or abnormal deliveries, as well as direct damage or injury through disease during the perinatal and neonatal periods.

The most common cases comprise the relatively large number of people in the community suffering varying degrees of cerebral palsy, from a minor spasticity of a hand or leg in its mildest form, to the involvement of all four limbs when it is severe. The locus of the damage in these cases is usually well known, and is frequently confined in a remarkably precise way to the motor areas concerned with general body movement.

One of the most significant questions which arise in this connection is how can it happen that individual brains can sustain this degree of insult while, at the same time, the complex processes subserving perception and learning often escape untouched? Yet happen it does, as the numerous severely disabled, often chair-ridden sufferers demonstrate, many of whom are holding down jobs demanding a high degree of intelligence and mental agility.

What is doubly surprising is the existence of these people alongside others who have no significant medical history of any kind, yet who are severely handicapped in formal learning through inadequate or defective perceptual skills.

Having said this, it is, of course, clear that not all people in the group sustaining gross brain damage have their learning potential left unimpaired. For some the consequences are profound, and they are left with little capacity for living anything approaching normal lives.

Another feature of this type of disability is its social acceptance in the community: that is, there is a generally sympathetic response to people who are seen to be suffering physical handicap. This contrasts dramatically with the widespread if understandable lack of sympathetic response to those whose disabilities are not immediately apparent, such as the partially hearing, but is also experienced by those who have learning problems of obscure or unknown origin. Their situation is made worse by the natural tendency of parents to resist the idea of anything being wrong and, in the absence of any visible evidence to think in terms of more acceptable explanations, such as a lack of inclination or effort.

When particularly massive damage occurs, who can say what ingenious adaptations some brains achieve in order to sustain life itself, let alone meet the demands of formal learning? Any living organism functions as a dynamic whole in dealing with its environment and will make the best possible adaptation to given circumstances. (A beetle, if its legs are unserviceable through injury, will propel itself using the mandibles of its lower jaw although, biologically, these organs were never designed to fulfil such a function.)

In fact, a common characteristic of individuals coping with life proscribed through brain damage in this way, is their will and determination to overcome their difficulties. People who have to grow up and live with severe disabilities often sustain a quality of life and achievement which confound even the most optimistic predictions which have been made regarding their future.

Minimal brain damage

This is the difficult area. Here no hard neurological signs exist to lead to an undisputed diagnosis. Indeed, to many neurologists minimal brain damage is not a useful concept and, without the hard evidence, for them no definable condition exists. (Not all of them agree: a notable exception being the late Macdonald Critchley, who wrote a number of books on Dyslexia.)

What has confused the issue more than anything else is the implied notion of structural damage. The brain is known to have massive compensatory resources, and to some neurologists the notion that something which, by definition, is minimal, can have such significant behavioural consequences is untenable for this reason.

In my view there has been a major error made in assuming an identity between certain aspects of brain function when, in fact, there are no logical grounds for doing so. We have assumed that the higher perceptual processes, which include within them the capacity to hold and to process symbolic data into the form required for learning, follow the same general rules as those which operate in other aspects of perception.

The evidence of the unimpaired perceptual skills in people who have sustained substantial structural damage to their brains, plus the evidence of these same skills in children suffering such severe genetic defects as mongolism, argues that these processes are dependent upon a physiological or neuro-physiological integrity of a different (not necessarily higher) order or nature. Indeed, it is daily becoming more probable that these anomalies will be found eventually to reside in abnormalities of a biochemical, rather than a structural or physical nature. It is for this reason more than any other that reference to organic damage, as against organic dysfunction, is not only undesirable on psychological and medical grounds; it is also wrongly conceived.

Associated with – not caused by

It is possible to draw inferences from case histories and to think in terms of their association with subsequent learning problems but, as has been mentioned earlier, the concept of association rather than any idea of a simple cause-effect relationship is of paramount importance.

Although all behaviour has to be viewed as dynamic and not stereotyped, it is particularly true of cognitive (mental) behaviour and, again, especially significant in cases where some factor intrudes adversely to affect learning behaviour. The poor attempts at decoding the words in a book by the poor reader are, themselves, aspects of behaviour – which may or may not imply an underlying condition. We are not looking at something tangible, like a hole in the head, but behavioural signs which may be indicating some underlying pathology. But we are not interested in the pathology for its own sake.

94

Epilepsy is a condition which manifests itself in a wide variety of behaviour disturbances, and surgical procedures sometimes show a locus of pathology with which the condition is associated. But the lesion is not the epilepsy. The epilepsy is the disordered behaviour and will have a variety of origins, although the observed patterns of behaviour may have a lot in common.

In the same way, learning disabilities will have a variety of origins and they will be of varying degrees of severity — from the most mild to the most severe. But there is no logic in giving them different names simply because they are different in degree.

If my child had a difficult birth does it mean that he will have a learning disability?
No.

For those directly concerned with the problem of severe learning difficulties in children it is clearly good professional practice, as well as simple common sense, to enquire into the circumstances of a child's early life, including the period of pregnancy, the situation and circumstances during confinement, and the baby's perinatal life, particularly the early hours and days. (See case histories.)

It does not mean that if your baby had a particularly traumatic birth or you yourself had problems in pregnancy, that he must inevitably encounter difficulties in development or in later learning. It does mean however that when such problems do arise the individual child can be deemed to have been at risk during that period, and should certainly be given the benefit of the doubt when discrepancies occur between his expected and actual performance. And, equally importantly, when behaviour problems rather than learning difficulties arise. Although this is not the place to discuss them, there can be no doubt that many of the behaviour and adjustment problems which reveal themselves, sometimes from an early age, have their origins in early histories of this kind.

Some medical and psychological authorities take the view that evidence of this kind, though obviously not discounted clinically, nevertheless has only academic interest, in the sense that there is nothing to be done about it. Without wishing to be unfair to them I have to say that such information is of far more than academic interest in other contexts. It is of value, and certainly preferable for parents to know that their child's difficulties could be, or even are, possibly associated with a significant birth history, rather than to be told that there is nothing wrong with him, that they are making a fuss about nothing or, worst of all, that he will grow out of it. Some parents have been waiting for this to happen for an awfully long time. It is also of value and important that a teacher should know that the difficulties a child is encountering in his learning, (or showing in his behaviour), could have their origins in a significant birth or early history, rather than assume that they are due to mismanagement or lack of care on the part of his parents. Lastly, it is of paramount importance, and simple justice, that the child should be recognised as a possible victim of such circumstances, rather than be deemed bloody-minded, lazy or plain stupid as they often are.

Is there anything we have done which has caused our child's problem?

Some parents — particularly mothers — express anxiety that something they might have done, or failed to do is the possible cause of their child's condition. Many more probably have such fears but never feel able to express them.

The first point to make has been mentioned earlier — that the incidence of these disabilities is no higher in one social group than another. It is possible that a higher proportion of children referred for investigation have professional parents, but this is almost certainly due to their greater preoccupation with their children's education than to any causal factor. The truth is that no degree of caring or quality of parenting has anything to do with these defects.

Some mothers recall an incident during pregnancy — usually unavoidable — which they dwell upon as, in their eyes, the time when things went wrong.

The likelihood of any such event being identifiable, even by a specialist, is extremely remote but, more important is the fact that in the majority of cases there is no history or evidence with which an association might be made. Additionally, children who do have such histories and in some cases have sustained brain injury have escaped such learning disabilities altogether.

The message must be that morbid preoccupation with the past is both negative and useless and all your interest and energy should be focused on the practical problem of improving your child's situation.

SUMMARY

● The important distinction between gross brain damage and minimal brain damage was emphasised.

● In cases of severe brain injury the processes of perception are often left unimpaired. Many people who have sustained such injury have done well educationally and followed successful careers.

● The subtle constitutional defects with which specific learning disabilities are associated have to be thought of in functional terms. It is probable that in many cases they have no structural features and are due to physiological and bio-chemical abnormalities.

● In cases where there has been early injury there is no simple cause and effect relationship between that injury and the subtle perceptual defects which affect learning. Although one child's learning disability may have a lot in common with another child's learning disability there are no grounds for assuming that they are both associated with identical events or conditions.

● Just as other behavioural abnormalities — such as epilepsy — can be mild or severe, so learning disabilities can be mild or severe. There is no logic in calling something by a different name when it is simply different in degree.

5

SENSORY DEFECTS – WHAT IF MY CHILD IS PARTIALLY HEARING OR PARTIALLY SIGHTED?

One of the chief anxieties for parents who discover that they have a deaf or partially-sighted child is over its implications for their formal education.

This short chapter is included mainly to reassure such parents that there is no reason for fearing that these children will necessarily have defects of central perceptual organisation of the kind we are discussing and that, consequently, they will be inefficient learners.

The quality and efficiency of our higher-order perceptual processes which subserve the learning of symbolic material – as in reading – are in no way determined by the quality or efficiency of our sensory apparatus.

It may at first sound inconceivable that a child with impaired hearing can have efficient auditory perception, or that a child with impaired sight can have efficient visual perception – but such is the case. Sensory perception, at the peripheral level – of the eyes or the ears – is determined by the efficiency of these organs in a mechanical sense. The higher, qualitatively different central perception, whereby the brain processes and organises the information coming in is what makes the sense data or information intelligible: and this function can be wholly unimpaired in children who have defective hearing or sight.

An indication of the significance and importance of central processing is seen in the way it makes use of information coming via different channels in order to supplement the limited information which may be available — as in the case of lip-reading in the deaf. Similarly, and more dramatically, it can use information coming in through alternative sensory channels, not biologically designed for the reception of symbolised information — as in the case of the blind child using his fingers to read Braille.

It would be foolish to dismiss or to fail to take full account of the degree of handicap a child with a sensory defect suffers: obviously he will be at a disadvantage in any learning situation — formal or otherwise. The important point I wish to make is that the child's capacity to organise and to use what sensory information he does receive operates quite independently of the channels of information themselves.

Many partially hearing children have efficient higher-order perceptual processes and learn to read with comparative ease, though their articulation and intelligibility are sometimes so poor that only those very closely acquainted with them are able to understand them. Their comprehension of what they are reading can very easily be established through their written work, or when their speech is sufficiently intelligible.

The fact is best illustrated via two case histories, through which parents of partially-hearing or partially-sighted children may be able to find reassurance, and be able to accept that defects of hearing or vision in young children do not necessarily isolate them from efficient learning and a good standard of educational achievement.

P.W. A partially-hearing child

P.W. was a profoundly deaf child of very high general ability who was first known to me in primary school and who, with the help of peripatetic teachers of the deaf was able to sustain herself in a normal school situation. She gained admission to a university course at nineteen and took a degree in fine arts.

In a recent discussion with her she was able to give me an account of her subjective experiences, and her own description

100

of how she coped with her problem in the early years.

It was clear that she first associated meaning with concrete objects e.g. a BALL. The ball existed for her as a percept in her head: not as a phoneme — (the sound of the word). Any concrete object, or any object she saw pictorially represented in a book together with the printed symbol BALL was represented in the same way. There was no corresponding phoneme to BALL in her head, only the knowledge that the round thing on the page, or in her hand to be played with, was represented by the visual symbol BALL. Hence she knew what the written word BALL meant long before she had any recognisable phoneme for it and, consequently, long before she was able to articulate the word.

Through learning isolated associations in this way, her vocabularly of nouns rapidly increased and, through using her high general intelligence she gradually acquired an understanding of other parts of speech — conjunction, verbs, adverbs — but only so long as there was a concrete situation represented which was meaningful for her, and with which she could then associate the written word. Thus the development of her decoding (reading) skill, followed a quite different course from that of hearing children and was probably similar to that followed by other severely deaf children.

The question now arises whether or not children with sensory deficits can suffer additionally from specific learning disabilities of the kind we are discussing: and the answer, of course, is yes.

Such children present a considerable problem to the various specialists who have to try to establish what their learning potential might be. Fortunately, with modern resources and techniques it is possible to determine in mechanical or physical terms a degree of hearing loss or visual defect with some accuracy. What then remains to be assessed is what level of general ability or intelligence the child has at his disposal, so that realistic educational expectations are established and appropriate demands made of him. This is not easy to do but, armed with suitable test batteries for partially-hearing or partially-sighted children it is possible for the psychologist to determine within reasonable limits their general ability level.

If with all this information the child still fails to make the expected progress, then he must be given the benefit of the doubt and be deemed to have additional perceptual disabilities. It is too facile, and would also be irresponsible to ascribe his failure to the single fact of his sensory defect, or to extraneous factors.

P.K. A partially-sighted child

A similar degree of higher-order sensory organisation and perception can be demonstrated in a partially-sighted child.

P.K. was visually a severely disabled girl who left her small village school to attend a school for partially-sighted pupils as soon as she was old enough to board.

In spite of her extremely impaired vision and with low-average general ability she encountered no serious difficulty in learning to read and has been a fluent reader for some years.

As with P.W. and her impaired hearing this girl's achievement demonstrates the independence of higher processes of organisation and perception from the quality of sensory information which is available.

P.K.'s reproduction of designs from memory (See Fig. 4) was made following the standard exposure time of ten seconds. She scanned the test card holding it some three or four inches from her eyes and was quite unable to distinguish the important features at a distance of one foot.

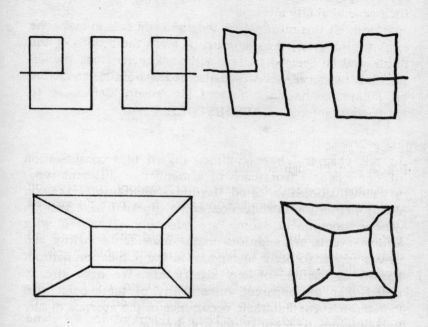

Fig. 4

Reproduction from memory of a partially-sighted girl of fifteen with myopia, nystagmus and albinism. (Vision: Left eye 4/60; Right eye 6/60.) Note that in this excellent overall perception is included the shift to the right of the inner rectangle: often not perceived by children of the same age with perfect visual acuity. P.K. attends a special school for the partially-sighted. She is of low-average intelligence and a fluent reader — holding the script some three or four inches from her eyes.

6

CASE HISTORIES

In this chapter I have confined myself to a consideration of one example from each of a number of different types of constitutionally based learning disabilities. As was mentioned in the introduction, some appear to have a strong genetic component, some are probably associated with known events or conditions in the individual's history and others appear to occur at random in the population without known association of any significance. We have already noted that the apparent vulnerability of these perceptual systems is such that their occurrence in the absence of any known traumatic event should not surprise us.

Case History 1: *Girl A.S. — A genetic disability.*

By far the most impressive case of a genetic disability — affecting a family through three generations — was discovered only recently. The child referred to me was a girl of eight years (A.S.) whose detailed history follows. What is of interest in this context is that she is the daughter of a woman who was one of ten children: four girls and six boys. Of these ten only two of the girls read without difficulty, the other two and the six boys being illiterate and remaining so into their adult lives.

All four girls married and are successful housewives and mothers. One of the brothers had a congenital eye condition and, though otherwise fit, has remained unemployed.

The other five brothers have established themselves in good jobs and continue to be employed as follows:

A motor mechanic.

A self-employed plasterer.

A long distance lorry driver.

A poultry processor.

Lastly — an exceptional success story — a senior employee with an internationally known firm who works in the agricultural side of their operations. He, as do the others, continues to be unable to read or write.

What is of further interest genetically, is that both the mother and grandmother of these children were quite unable to read or write, indicating (unusually — as the incidence is generally believed to be in the region of four males to one female), that the transmission was on the female side.

A.S. is a charming, sensitive eight-year-old girl with an IQ of 114. She is a non-reader.

She walked at fourteen months and was an early talker, (at one year), with excellent articulation. She went to play-school at three and enjoyed it.

She has been seen by a neurologist and no abnormality was detected.

Currently she is sleeping badly and constantly worried about her performance at school. She often cries in bed and, on one occasion there said to her mother, "Will I ever be able to read? (Mary) can read, why can't I?"

She loves doing practical things and her puppet making, pottery and painting are all of a high order.

Although she is being sensitively managed, both at home and at school, the implicit and unavoidable pressures on this highly motivated child have caused us to proceed with her ascertainment as a handicapped pupil and to make provision for her outside the normal school. (Ideally it would have been preferable to provide for her in the normal school but, occasionally, when a child is not sufficiently resilient emotionally — as in A.S.'s case — it is necessary to look to alternatives.

Case History 2: *Boy T.A. — A mother's account.*

T.A. was born during the blitz in hospital weighing five pounds five ounces — an induced (not premature) birth. He was difficult to feed and this lack of interest in food persisted for years — perhaps because wartime food was monotonous, with no fresh fruit, eggs, sweets or chocolate to stimulate his appetite. He developed normally, never crawling, but progressing 'on all fours'. He walked just after his first birthday and was very active and fastidious, refusing to keep on a wet napkin. He talked early, having a normal conversation by the age of two.

Air-raids persisted — we lived in Surrey in the flight path of enemy flying bombs and rockets, so I could not allow him too far afield, but he was not nervous.

At three he was toppled over by a large Old English Sheepdog and was so frightened that this fear of dogs lasted until 1978, although we tried to help him by buying him a puppy, this was too boisterous for him.

When I was pregnant in 1945, we had to arrange for him to go to a nursery in Sevenoaks as it was too dangerous to take him to London to his grandparents, and my husband was still in the Navy. This experience was shattering to T.A.

He was always quick at understanding and good with his hands, although there were no educational toys to buy. He went to a village school and was quite happy (except at dinner time). He liked stories being read, but I could not get him to read at all easily. When he sat for public school entrance at seven and a half he failed at reading, but was accepted on his other tests.

He did not progress in, nor like, subjects that related to reading, but was good at maths, was crazy about chemistry and was always interested in biology. He did not like team games, probably because with his very slight build he suffered in the rough and tumble of football.

At 'O' level, he failed English three times, but went as a trainee chemist to the Atomic Station in Harwell and did very well there. It was in research at Harwell that he transferred to the medical division and changed his course from chemistry to medicine. He went on to medical school and qualified as a doctor.

T.A. is an interesting example of a highly intelligent individual who, through using his ability and drive, managed to overcome his disability sufficiently to establish himself in a successful professional career.

A significant feature is his continuing inability to process certain types of information efficiently. Logically, anyone with the ability to function efficiently as a General Practitioner should not consciously have to struggle to retain the briefest of telephone numbers, yet this is, in fact, the case.

Whatever component of the auditory processing system was absent or defective in his childhood, apparently continues to be so.

Case History 3: *Boy L.H.K. – An atypical and significant birth history.*

L.H.K. was born twenty weeks into an apparently healthy pregnancy, mother being diagnosed as suffering from a chill on the bladder. He was 2lb 12oz at birth and spent the first three months in an incubator. He then went home from hospital weighing 5lbs. He sat up at eighteen months; he weighed 14lbs at one year of age. He had numerous illnesses up to five years of age, and at many points was not expected to survive.

He walked at two and a half and talked when he was four years.

At seven years and nine months he was referred to me by his head teacher because of his failure to learn.

At this time, I described L.H.K. as follows:

'a bright responsive little boy. He was very positive in his behaviour and obviously highly motivated.

107

He is of just average ability, obtaining an IQ of 92 on the Stanford-Binet L—M Scale. His attainments generally fall far below the expected level.

This boy's test record reveals an extremely poor auditory perception and memory, together with a less defective, but significantly poor visual memory. These factors combine to make him seriously handicapped educationally, and undoubtedly account for his poor formal attainments.'

At ten years L.H.K. was admitted to an excellent boarding school catering for slow learners, where he had all the advantages of small classes, plus the individual and intensive help that such an environment could provide. Despite this, when he was seen at fifteen years four months, prior to the Leavers' Conference, he was still, effectively, a non-reader. His performance on the test of auditory perception was as follows:

Repeating Digits

    (a) 3 – 1 – 8 – 5 – 9   3 – 8 – – – – – –

    (b) 4 – 8 – 3 – 7 – 2   – – – – – – – –

    (c) 9 – 6 – 1 – 8 – 3   9 – 6 – – – – – –

Thus, with an IQ that had remained essentially constant, and within the low average to average range over eight years, plus the advantages of a special learning environment, he never achieved a commensurate level of formal attainments.

The interesting features of this test profile are that his vocabulary score was at the average level, as was his score on the Ingenuity sub-test, while he failed the repeating of digits test — at the seven year level — being able to repeat only two of the five digits given.

L.H.K. is probably the best example I have come across of a child who has specific learning disabilities, probably associated with a significant birth history, adversely and seriously affecting all areas of his learning while his intelligence level remained at the low average to average level.

He is now settled in manual employment and is highly thought of as an able and conscientious worker.

NOTE

I would emphasise that this case history is included as an extreme example of a specific learning disability in a child of good general intelligence. It should be stressed that such cases are rare, but their existence demonstrates that, in terms of severity of handicap, there is no limit to what these disabilities represent.

It should not be overlooked that L.H.K. had a significant medical history with which his disability was almost certainly associated. The chances of any problem of this severity occurring without such association are remote.

Case History 4: *Boy — A fairly typical case history: again with a significant genetic component.*

A.L. was referred to me at eight and a half years as a non-reader. I found him to be of average ability (IQ: 99) and described him as:

'an intelligent looking, responsive child. His test record contains evidence of a very defective auditory perception (he is able to repeat only three digits). On the other hand, his visual perception is average for his age.'

Mother's Account

When A.L. was a little baby, he seemed to be over-active. He did not need much sleep and he was on the go the whole time. All the baby stages of development he passed very quickly, and he was forward in everything except his speech. He would never be able to repeat a new word exactly right, often he would just say half of a word and, of course, it was a long time before anyone could understand him. Even now at eleven years old he doesn't speak clearly, and often uses only the tail end of words.

Very early A.L. seemed to thirst for knowledge, he would ask question after question, and he would learn very quickly. Often he would pick things up without being told. This is the reason we couldn't understand why he came to a dead stop when he started school. G. (father) and A.L. are both the same in this. They enjoy television shows like *Survival,* documentaries and all programmes which are informative on current affairs and natural history. A.L. benefits a lot from these, because he is learning without the struggle of reading for himself.

G. is a slow reader, but he plods on through book after book of serious subjects like history, geography, science, etc., as well as pilot exams, but he still can't relax now he's flying because he has great difficulty when repeating messages on the radio about navigation and direction. He always has to check and double check when looking at dials in the cockpit because he has the tendency to read things back to front.

Both G. and A.L. are good with their hands. G. puts his skills into building and A.L. is finding that he also seems to have a flair in this direction too. A.L. in very interested in art and craft at school and he always comes up with some wonderful ideas about things to make.

G. is a quick learner and a hard worker, but at school he was told that he was dense and stupid and that he would never make anything of himself. He had a very hard time at school, in trouble all the time out of frustration and he finally taught himself to read out of comic strips like Dan Dare. Personally I think that to do this would be so much harder than the ordinary way we learn, and I can't see why, if their brains are capable of learning the hard way, they can't learn the ordinary simpler way.

There is a dyslexia type problem in the men of my husband's family. His father, grandfather and two brothers have all had difficulties. It is hard to tell what the exact troubles are because they all had a poor education and, because they were slow learners, they were put in a corner at the back of the class and forgotten about. We can only be thankful that these problems are recognised nowadays and that there are such good teachers who are helping children with these special difficulties. I feel that A.L. will make his way through life much better now that he has the backing of these experienced teachers within the education system.

In Chapter 3 there was some discussion on the significance of scatter in a child's performance. This made particular reference to the fact that some children of good general ability frequently fail on specific tasks of auditory and visual perception. They are usually inefficient learners with formal attainments well below the expected level. Case History 5 is an excellent example of such a child.

Case History 5: *Boy M.J.L.*

He was first referred to me as a seven-year-old when he was found to have an IQ of 104. Subsequent tests have confirmed his average ability, together with relatively very poor attainments. A detailed breakdown of his most recent performance (September, 1982) is given, as it is the best way of illustrating the significance of these deficits in an otherwise intelligent child.

No conditions or events could be identified in M.J.L.'s history with which his poor perception and consequent learning disability could be associated.

M.J.L. Seen at School 16.9.82. Stanford-Binet L—M Scale: IQ = 104. All sub-tests passed at six year level.

Year Seven:	all sub-tests passed except repeating of five digits. He also failed on three sets of four digits, succeeding with three only reliably.
Year Eight:	all sub-tests passed, including:
	Vocabulary: 8+ words required: *14 given.*

Year Nine:	Memory for designs: failed (see figure).
	Rhymes: failed (two given out of three).
	Giving change (mental subtraction):
	a) 12 - 4 *8* b) 24 - 10 *14*
	Repeating 4 digits reversed: failed.
Year Ten:	three sub-tests passed out of four:
	Vocabulary: 11 words required: 14 given.
	Abstract words: Curiosity; surprise
	Curiosity . . . "wants to know what's happening."
	Surprise . . . "something turns up."
	Word naming: 28 required: 33 given.
	Repeating 6 digits: failed.
Year Eleven:	Three sub-tests passed of four required.
	Memory for designs: (Higher level) failed (see fig.).
	Verbal absurdities: (2) passed.
	Abstract words: 3 required, 5 given.
	Notable responses:
	c) Conquer . . . "win a battle."
	d) Obedience . . . "doing what teacher tells you."
	e) Revenge . . . "if you killed someone's grandad and he got put in gaol he'd come out and get revenge on you."
	Similarities: Three things (3+ required):
	a) A snake - a cow - a sparrow . . . "all move."
	b) A rose - a potato - a tree . . . "grow in the soil."
	c) Wool - cotton - leather . . . "used to make things."
Year Twelve:	one sub-test passed of four required.
	Vocabulary: 15 words required: 14 given — failed.
	Verbal absurdities: 4 required, 5 given — passed.
	Abstract words: failed.

                    Sentence completion: failed.
Year Thirteen: three sub-tests passed of four required.
                    Plan of search: passed.
                    Abstract words: 4 required: 5 given.
                    Problems of fact: (2) passed.
                    Dissected sentences: omitted (non-reader)
                    – failed.

Thus M.J.L.'s distribution of successes and failures range over nine years of mental-age-achieved as follows:

	months	
Year Six:	12	(basal age)
Year Seven:	9	
Year Eight:	12	
Year Nine:	3	
Year Ten:	9	
Year Eleven:	9	
Year Twelve:	3	
Year Thirteen:	9	
Year Fourteen:	0	

                              10 years 6 months

M.J.L. is typical of the group of children who have generally inadequate perception – both visually and auditorily. The failures in his text performance invariably refer to tasks which make demands on both modes of perception in a specific sense (see figures), and not on general reasoning ability. His impressive performance in year thirteen (3 sub-tests correct out of 4), at ten years and one month of age, is significant in this connection. All his successes involved reasoning ability; his one failure was on a task which involved reading and was therefore omitted.

   That many of these children are acutely aware of their situation and protect themselves through flights into fantasy is borne out by M.J.L.'s remarks:

"I was head of everybody on that book. I was on fifty-something; the others were on thirty. I was doing a page every day and they were ever-so hard."

M.J.L. has a reading age of barely six years — effectively a non-reader for a child of his age.

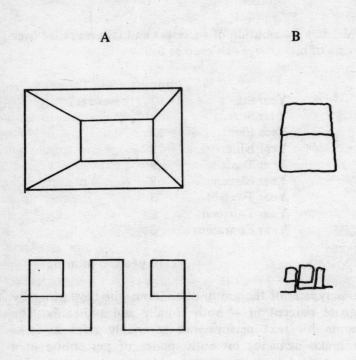

Fig. 5.
M.J.L.'s reproduction of designs.

7

WHAT CAN I DO TO HELP?

What should my attitude be?

The first essential is to get the situation into perspective for yourself and especially for your child. If he has the misfortune to be an inefficient learner it is not the end of the world and it can do immense harm to his self-confidence and self-esteem if your behaviour and attitude suggest otherwise. The first positive contribution you can make therefore is to take stock of your values and priorities, and to make sure that your concern is for your child's welfare in the widest sense, and not confined to a preoccupation with his school performance.

Try standing back from the situation to get a better perspective of what his current difficulties mean, against the background of his whole personality and his capacity to make a good and self-fulfilling life for himself. If necessary, and as part of this exercise, set out consciously to cultivate or refurbish your sense of humour (as it may well have received a battering), and encourage your child to develop his own. He will find this easier to do if the heat can be taken out of the situation and he is helped to see his problem more objectively and in a wider perspective. It is not enough to tell him that all you expect and want is that he should do his best. This is a hideously unspecific and demanding expectation to impose on anybody. What he needs to know is that you are aware of and accept that there are limits set on what he will achieve in the short-term, in spite of his own best efforts.

It is an appalling irony if some well-meaning but misguided professional person leaves you with the impression that if only you had observed your child more closely or, if only you had acted and sought advice when you noticed some tell-tale signs, something could have been done about it. To imply that this is so is indefensible and totally wrong. If any problem your child encounters is associated with a disability of constitutional origin then, by definition, it is not due to your mismanagement or neglect. Equally, it would not have been made to go away by any measures you might have taken.

Try to suppress any tendency you might have to be too concerned about your child's development. If his needs are conspicuous, you, as a caring parent will notice them soon enough. Sensory defects — such as poor hearing — are the sort of thing it is possible to overlook, and this is an area where early detection is important and special provision can make a dramatic difference to a child's educational potential. With perceptual disabilities on the other hand, even if we are able to establish their existence at a very early age — which I believe to be impossible — there are no preventive or practical measures you can take to help, over and above giving him a good physical and emotional environment in which to develop.

Don't look for scapegoats. If you can accept that your child's situation is not due to neglect or mismanagement on your part, then, neither is it due to neglect or mismanagement on the part of others — specifically his teachers or the education authority.

It may well be that the onus of doing something about it does rest with the authoriy but, in terms of your attitude to the problem it is important to distinguish between what is a fact of life over which no one has any control and, on the other hand, the practical problem it represents in terms of appropriate educational provision and management.

There is nothing to be gained in feeling bitter and having thoughts of recrimination. The problem is a shared one between you and the education authority, and you both have a vested interest in seeing to it that it is dealt with in a practical and effective way.

As was discussed earlier, the 1981 Education Act has, as one of its main objectives, the involvement of parents in the whole process of identifying and providing for special educational needs. It will be better for your child and for those with special needs generally if your energies are not dissipated in fostering discontent and pressing for educational provisions outside the main-stream of education. My chief reason for advocating this is, quite simply, that there is nothing so special about what your child needs that it cannot be provided within his own school. It is this provision that you should be pressing for and which can and will be made available. If only because no Local Education Authority can afford to ignore the fact that specifically learning-disabled children comprise a significant proportion of the slow learners in their schools.

Accept and love your child unconditionally. If you are unable to come to terms with his problem at an emotional level it is unlikely that he will manage to do it himself. The quality of his adjustment to his situation is bound to be largely determined by your own, so, make sure that what feelings of frustration you have yourself are not communi-cated to him as disappointment or disapproval. Encourage him to see and delight in the things he can do well, even if, as will sometimes be the case, these things have to be mainly non-academic. Better still, start by seeing them in this light yourself.

It is high time that society generally, but parents in particular, gave up the idea that academic success is the only kind of success there is for young people. With the social and economic structure and demands of society changing so rapidly, there are all kinds of skills and attributes which are going to be required to meet these different needs and which will come to be more highly valued. Craft and art skills for small businesses, skill in all kinds of sport, practical care for

117

old people in the community, the constructive use of leisure as an end in itself: all these are going to have a new status and meaning in this developing, technological age.

Should I speak to his teacher?

If you genuinely believe that your child has learning potential which is not being realised there can be no question that your first priority should be an approach to his teacher. You are entitled to access to his teacher although, quite properly, head-teachers have the right to decide how and when such a meeting shall take place, and there are bound to be local variations. The point you should understand is that you do have this right of access and, as you will discover, this is not only available to you but actively encouraged in most cases. All that you are generally asked to do is to take advantage of and to follow the procedure of the individual school.

When you meet his teacher you should try to bear certain things in mind.

Firstly, his teacher is not there by accident. She is following a chosen profession which implies at the very least an interest in and usually a love of children. She would not have elected to spend her working life in their company if this were not the case.

Secondly, she wants to succeed as a teacher. There is no joy for her in failing to apply her skills or in spending her days confronted with bored, uninterested and failing children. The only measure of her success is their success.

Thirdly, she wants your child to succeed. The children around her who are fortunate in being efficient learners and who soak up knowledge like blotting paper are satisfying to her in some respects, but they don't stretch her as a teacher. They don't cause her to examine closely what she is doing or to ask herself how she might do it better. If your child has a learning disability, he does. It is meeting him and the problem he presents as a teaching task that makes her job worthwhile and rewarding in a special way. She gets more

118

satisfaction from breaking through and achieving some success with a child who is encountering difficulty than she does in commending the work of the good achievers. (If you find that difficult to believe it would probably be good for you to overhear some of her conversations with her colleagues in the staff-room.)

Lastly, she is often acutely aware of and distressed by the frustrations of your child. She knows that every child wants to succeed: to please his parents, to please her even, but most of all to have the feeling of self-esteem that only success brings. She gets no pleasure, in fact you can be sure that she feels pain at his constant failure, and is more concerned about this than her own or your situation.

Bearing these things in mind, go and talk to her. Without being offensive or critical you can show her your anxiety and seek her views on the problem in an atmosphere of mutual concern, and with a clear understanding on both sides that you each want the same thing: your child to succeed.

You may discover that you are largely if not totally in agreement with each other. She may be just as convinced as you are that your child has general ability or intelligence well above what is reflected in his work.

On the other hand, you must be prepared to find yourself in disagreement. She may take the view — quite responsibly — that your assessment of your child's ability is not realistic, and that your aspirations for him in terms of his learning potential are wildly optimistic. Be prepared for this.

In any event, either by agreement or without agreement you can approach your child's head teacher and make a formal request that he be seen by an educational psychologist for assessment and a professional opinion on his educational situation and needs in a comprehensive way. You have a right to this service and, provided your concern is sincere you can be confident that an objective opinion will be available to you.

Why should I take the long view?

Invariably, when talking to parents of children whose educational progress is frustrated by reason of a specific learning disability, I find myself eventually encouraging them to take the long view of his educational career and possible achievements.

This does not mean that they and his teachers should sit back and wait for things to happen; but it does mean that, having secured all the constructive advice and assistance available, they should set their eyes on long-term rather than short-term goals.

Once again one has to caution against generalisation. An individual's progress will always be slower or swifter according to the degree of his disability, but it is still necessary to avoid the attractive but treacherous assumption made by some parents that, given the extra or specialist help, his progress will now be normal and he will achieve the full range of achievement commensurate with his intelligence. Additionally, by not being in too much of a hurry, they will give the child the best possible chance of realising his potential, without his energies being drawn off in emotional conflict and argument between themselves, or with his teachers.

Also, as a consequence of this attitude, rather than as an objective in itself, his achievement will be all the greater if his attempt to obtain some formal qualification occurs when he is somewhat more mature generally. If he is pressed into examinations with his age group there is a risk that he might fail, when, with an extra year or so he would stand a much better chance of doing justice to himself. I refrain from saying full justice, because the reality of the situation is that this is something he might never achieve. The aim should be to prepare him to meet educational demands when the chances of his performing well are optimal.

I can almost hear the cry from some parents and teachers that this option of delay in an attempt at obtaining basic qualifications, or access to higher education, is not open to them. Public examinations, CSE's, 'O' levels and 'A' levels all come at a predetermined time. My glib, but honest, response is, so what?

There is no doubt that we, in this country, have become conditioned to accepting a standardised educational progression as a fact of life. We have come to accept the educational framework and programme for any child from five to sixteen years or eighteen years as inviolate. A framework in which a child either takes his opportunities and achieves, and is therefore a success, or loses out and is a failure.

This need not be the case.

Many young people would achieve far more, both in formal educational terms and in terms of a satisfying career, if they, and their parents, were encouraged to take a less rigid view of their education and a more positive attitude to what they might achieve on a different time scale.

All kinds of opportunities are available, up to and including pursuing courses of higher education well after school leaving age.

Parents may have to face the reality that their child is not academic in the traditional sense. It does not mean that he is incapable of achieving other things, or even the same things over a longer period of time.

Some parents may have had successful educational careers themselves and feel that they are justified in having expectations that their children will do equally well. This is not how things are — as earlier discussion in this book has tried to show.

On the other hand, if a child has the general ability to do well, then only two things are required: patience and motivation. Patience on everyone's part, and strong motivation in the child.

Given this combination, there is no reason why a child should not achieve to the limit of, or near to the limit of, his intelligence level, in the long term. He might well suffer acute frustration on the way; he might well have to suffer the tedium of taking examinations more than once; he might even be advised by some of his mentors to reconsider his situation and intentions in the light of repeated failure. But, if he has the motivation, he will succeed.

It goes without saying that this motivation has to come from within. You cannot make your child motivated, and one of the greatest mistakes parents can make is to assume that their strong desires that he will do this, that or the other, can literally be transferred to him. Indeed, when their feelings and attitudes are excessively intense, they can have a negative effect and cause him to react in opposition to them. He has got to want to do it for himself and, if he wants it enough, he will not allow a specific learning disability to frustrate him in his long-term aims.

Finally, make a point of advising him on how to cope with his problem in the widest sense. How to cope with the social and emotional stresses which arise from, or will be associated with his situation as a slow learner. Help him to understand that it is too much to expect all teachers to be patient and understanding all of the time. There will be times when they are irritable and insensitive, or possibly just plain forgetful, and when they will fail to take account of his special needs. Help him to face up to the fact that he's got a problem and, like some other children, many of whom are more handicapped than he is, he has got to learn to cope with it.

It can even be seen in a positive light. By finding the will and determination to surmount his difficulties, he may, in so doing, equip himself to achieve more than some who are not handicapped in any way, and who find no spur to realise fully the abilities they have.

What can I do in a practical way?

The first rule must be: DON'T TRY TO GO IT ALONE.

Above all, don't be misled into thinking that by going out and buying expensive books and materials for your child to use at home you will necessarily be helping him with his problem. Books and materials in these situations are secondary to the right kind of attitude and a readiness to work with the child. No expensive remedial programme is of any value if he is left to flounder with it on his own. He must be able to understand what he is about and he must succeed in it.

Get to know his remedial teacher and be guided by her in what you do. Ideally, this will probably directly supplement what she herself is doing in the classroom.

Far too much has been said and written regarding the highly specialised help needed by specifically learning disabled children. What they need is certainly special, but not in the sense that this is usually understood. Once a reliable diagnosis of specific learning disability has been made, the major criteria which have to be met in regard to effective help are:

(i)   that it be given frequently.
(ii) that short-term and, if necessary, only very modest learning objectives are established.
(iii) that the child has continuing experience of success.

In regard to frequency of help it really does need to be given on a daily basis to give the best chance of achieving good results. For this reason, it is sometimes productive if the special teaching the child is receiving at school is supplemented by extra help in the home — his teacher is the best judge of this — providing always that it can be given in a relaxed atmosphere, free of emotional involvement on your part, and free of anxiety and apprehension on the part of the child.

One of the most useful features of this sort of help is that it can have complete continuity with what is being done in the classroom. If you can make youself known to your child's remedial teacher, and show an interest in and readiness to further the work she is doing, you will be getting — or rather your child will be getting — the best of both worlds.

Ask her if she will allow you to sit-in on some sessions when she is teaching your child. She will be pleased that you are keen to observe what she is doing and that you are prepared to learn from her. Also, it will be so much easier for her to communicate information about your child's particular difficulties and about how she is tackling them.

If her only contact with you is via a termly school-report or the occasional parents' evening, there will be little chance of your getting a clear idea of what is going on. And, by having an on-going involvement and relationship with his teacher, you will give your child the confidence of knowing that you are both on the same side and are making combined efforts to help him; as opposed to conveying insults to each other, often via the child who, as piggy-in-the-middle, is not going to be well placed or disposed to work effectively himself.

In regard to learning objectives: short-term, modest objectives are the key to success. Sometimes, when a child's disability is severe – it is necessary to be content with very small increments of progress: even of the order of mastering only a few words each week in some cases. The important thing, the essential thing, in fact, is that he succeeds in the tasks which are set him.

What these tasks will be, will be determined by the programme his remedial teacher has adopted to meet his peculiar needs. These can and do vary: and there is nothing wrong in this. Different teachers have different preferences for schemes of work and material, which they, as individuals, find most effective. There is no law which says they should all be doing the same thing, nor is there any evidence that one, and only one programme of work would be right for your child.

The criterion is, if it works, use it.

Some parents are very taken with the idea of homework, almost, it seems as an end in itself. But there is no merit in homework unless it has continuity with what is going on at school and, above all, the child knows what he is about.

This is an area where all teachers have a major responsibility. If they are going to set homework they should make sure that the child both understands what he has to do and that he is capable of doing it. Anything else is a pointless exercise.

Too many children bring home assignments which might as well be written in Serbo-Croat for all it means to them. If their return offerings are equally obscure, the blame can hardly rest with them.

This problem is more common at the secondary level, where subject-teachers are understandably identified with their own subjects and with the progress their pupils make in them.

It is impossible for a learning-disabled child to perform adequately across the whole curriculum and parents should therefore make sure that a realistic programme, tailored to his particular needs and educational objectives is agreed upon. It goes without saying that all teachers in a school should be aware of such a child's disability, and should make modified and realistic demands on him.

Communication is everything. Parents can make a major contribution to their child's effective learning by maintaining good relations with teachers and by ensuring that their expectations of him, and his teachers demands of him afford him a realistic chance of success.

8

IMPLICATIONS FOR TEACHERS AND LOCAL
EDUCATION AUTHORITIES

When a parent cries "My child isn't stupid" what does it
mean? What are the implications for his teachers and the
education authority? How has such a state of affairs come
about if — to take a common sense view — all those concerned
with his education want him to succeed? Surely no administrators in an education department, no head-teacher or any
member of staff can take pleasure in the failure of any child.
Teachers often express much the same sort of frustration
as parents: "Why is this child failing? We would help him if
we could."

One difficulty is that teachers do not yet fully understand
the true nature and effect on a child's learning of specific
disabilities of constitutional origin of the kind we have been
discussing. They have been firmly schooled in the tradition
that good teaching is the answer to everything. If one of their
(apparently bright) pupils is failing, they are bound to be
cautious about taking the view that the major part of the
problem lies within the child. Personality factors intrude
into this sort of situation and, however ill-advised, such
children are seen by some teachers as challenges to be met
and overcome — at whatever cost to themselves or the child.
Also, they don't want to do the child a disservice by taking
the risk of having someone say he is dull — when they know
he isn't. Equally, they may know the parents and be aware
of their anxieties, (sometimes wholly irrational fears that
their child could be hauled off to a special school), and do

not wish to initiate a procedure which might cause them further distress.

In some cases parents make it clear to teachers that they are totally against their child being 'seen' by anybody. They know he is all right, and if his teacher gets on with her job of teaching him — and does it properly — there will be no problem.

Because the subject of dyslexia has had such a bad press in educational circles, many teachers, psychologists and others view the whole subject of specific learning disabilities with some suspicion and tend to see any identification with it on their part as risky and ill-advised. Also, in fairness, it should be said that some educational psychologists (but a rapidly decreasing number), have had difficulty in conscientiously making a diagnosis of specific learning disability on professional grounds. Even worse, the dyslexia lobby has, perhaps unwittingly, diverted attention from the less than average but still eminently educable children who have equally severe disabilities, and who constitute a significantly large group in normal schools; many of them highly motivated and hard-working children. They are not scholars; they are not destined for higher education but, teachers know that, given the opportunity, the children of this grey area can achieve creditable formal attainments and become fulfilled and useful members of the community.

Because of this teachers react strongly against the singling out of an individual child simply as a consequence of the effort made by concerned and particularly determined parents to secure for him the provision they think he needs. The fact that they know that among the children they are responsible for, there are others who have equal or greater special needs is the main factor in this reaction and, understandably, may cause them to feel resentful. They know that if some of the children they are particularly concerned about had equally caring and articulate parents, they would be hearing a great deal more from them.

The 1944 Education Act

The 1944 Education Act contained a clause which has become a popular dictum, used whenever a suitable opportunity arises, − every child shall be educated . . . "according to his age, ability and aptitude'. A worthy objective, but more easily expressed than achieved.

In 1944 the implied requirement of determining what precisely were a child's 'ability and aptitude' did not appear to present any particular problem and, given the goodwill and co-operation of education authorities it appeared that this objective could be attained without much difficulty.

Where children were slow-learners the School Health Service, together with educational psychologists (where they were employed), would carry out the apparently straight-forward procedures of determining whether a child was 'educable' or not and, if educable, whether he was 'educationally subnormal' and in need of special provision − usually in a special school − or could be catered for in the mainstream of education. Children deemed to be ineducable were allocated places in training centres where they were sympathetically cared for and 'trained' to be socially competent to whatever standard they were capable of attaining, without any educational provision in a narrow or formal sense.

Now, happily, these establishments are properly designated schools ('no child is ineducable'), and are staffed by qualified teachers and welfare assistants.

A child deemed to be educationally sub-normal, that is whose IQ was above the severely limited range but not high enough for him to be suitably placed in a normal school was generally admitted to a special school − mostly to day schools in larger towns or cities − but frequently to boarding schools in rural areas.

In any community there will be a large number of 'slow-learning' children (in the region of twenty per cent of the school population), and education authorities still have the problem of selecting from these and providing for each child the best possible learning environment and teaching provision its resources will allow. Even without financial restraints this procedure of selection would never be easy.

The time has long gone when selection was based on the single criterion of a child's IQ. Even if we were able to regard this quotient as something immutable — as we once did — we know from experience that there is no direct relationship between this index and the true learning potential of any given child. Thus the task for any education authority of making educationally appropriate provision, and allocating equitable resources to all its children is a challenging one.

Firstly there is the problem of identification.

In the rather simplistic terms of the 1944 Act it appeared to be possible to identify the slow learner simply by reference to his IQ, but two anomalies have emerged in regard to this. Firstly, many of these slow learning children have shown themselves to be very efficient learners: that is, they are working effectively to the limits of their ability and there is no discrepancy between their expected and actual achievement. It follows from this that no clear need for a special learning environment for them is indicated — except possibly on social and/or emotional grounds. Secondly, it has become equally clear that a quite separate but significantly large group of slow-learners are failing to make acceptable progress for reasons other than low general ability. These are our specifically learning-disabled children.

Neither the Ministry of Education (as it then was), nor any education authority could have anticipated these events which have emerged gradually over the intervening years. In particular, they could not have envisaged the veritable hornet's nest which was always lying in wait and which was to become increasingly disturbed through the natural evolutionary process of improving educational provision.

Efforts to improve reading standards in particular, have been made, with most education authorities carrying out extensive surveys and screening procedures. (These consist in giving standardised tests of reading ability to all the children of a specific age group and assessing their performance against established norms or standards for that age group.) Also, individual researchers and teacher/writers have produced a great deal of relevant information and provided an impressive variety of special reading schemes and remedial material, aimed at assisting the child who is having difficulty in learning to read.

This concentration on reading standards has had unforeseen if inevitable consequences. It has set a premium on literacy on the one hand and has also caused some parents to see their authority as failing to meet the needs of their children because it, in their assessment, is not enabling them to achieve desired and expected results.

The truth is that no education authority could have anticipated or adequately prepared itself to meet what is, in effect, a new area of need. Nor could they have predicted the consequences of the continuing misuse of the term dyslexia — not only by the general public but, less excusably, by some professional people.

This has led to an accumulation of bad faith and mistrust when, all the time, the principals on both sides of the argument have had good and legitimate cases to make. It is only the inherent ambiguity of the term dyslexia itself which has caused the mischief and, but for this, teachers, parents and administrators could all have been engaged together in making better educational provision for this group of children.

Whereas the 1944 Act assumed fairly clear definitions and categories of handicap and the government proceeded to make appropriate educational provision to cater for children suffering these handicaps in suitable special schools, it has also become increasingly clear that this policy had some unforeseen inadequacies and defects.

One of the unfortunate consequences was the separating out and segregation of these children from the community of normal children in ordinary schools. This has caused us to view them mainly in terms of their handicaps and to demote their status as essentially normal children — in terms of their social and broad educational needs — who happened to be suffering some kind of disability.

Another thing the 1944 Act did not do, and could not have done at the time, was anticipate the presence in the school population of the large number of children who were not handicapped in the traditional sense but who, nevertheless, were learning-disabled to a significant degree. Certainly to a degree requiring special educational provision.

The 1981 Education Act

Although this book was begun before the provisions of the Act were known, it is encouraging to find that one of the basic aims of the book is very much in line with the spirit of the Act. That is in the sense that the Act concentrates on providing for the educational needs of children, rather than on making efforts to cater for types and degrees of educational handicap which may or may not exist.

There are a large number of specifically disabled children, but not all of them are dyslexic — and certainly would not be labelled as such under the new legislation. Even the classic 'dyslexic' should and, happily, will now be viewed along with all other disabled children as having recognisable and special educational needs.

Another major and welcome effect of the Act is that parents will be more directly involved in the discussions and decision making in regard to special educational provision for their children.

The task of making appropriate provision for every child is not an easy one and the involvement of parents at as early a stage as possible can only result in better informed and more appropriate measures being taken. Being more directly involved will also have the effect of giving them greater confidence in the authority's desire to determine and to provide for the educational needs of their children in a spirit

131

of co-operation and good faith.

A specific right under the Act which many parents will welcome but which, hopefully, will not be abused, is that of making a request to their authority that their child's educational needs are assessed. This clearly is intended to be done responsibly and where there is a genuine belief on the parents' part that the child might have special educational needs.

This right does not refer only to children of school age but extends to children from two to sixteen years — also to registered pupils at schools up to their nineteenth birthday.

Additionally, the Act empowers the LEA to assess the educational needs of children under the age of two years — with the parents consent — and it requires the authority to make an assessment if the parents ask for it.

Apart from major physical and mental handicaps very young children can show a variety of developmental difficulties, some of which may well be constitutional in origin. They could include speech-defects, motor-coordination problems, general clumsiness, hyperactivity etc., all of which should receive investigation and treatment as appropriate.

There are bound to be minor local variations in provision — as a consequence of differing locations, varying degrees of access to services as well as the inherent differences in schools themselves, their physical size, numbers on roll etc. On the whole however the Act is timely and will have particular benefits for the children who are the subject of this book.

Although all efforts should be made to mitigate a child's learning problems as they reveal themselves it is wrong to think in terms of simplistic solutions which are implied in such statements as: ' . . . early diagnosis and intervention are essential'. In the case of specific learning disabilities which are associated with subtle weaknesses in sensory organisation and consequent perceptual anomalies it is just not possible to make early and confident predictions of what a child's long-term educational needs are going to be. And it is wrong to give parents the idea that 'if only' there had been earlier identification of a problem their child would have been significantly less disadvantaged.

It should go without saying, but nevertheless should be stressed, that this does not refer to identifiable sensory and physical defects, where early diagnosis and attention can be of definitive importance.

Inevitably there have been cases where early signs of a learning disability have not been picked up. But this is not the reason that many intelligent children are late readers. As is discussed in the text, there are definite limits set on what the more severely disabled children will achieve in the short-term. What they will achieve will mainly depend upon arduous, painstaking effort over a period of time, and will not be significantly affected by some early dramatic intervention. And it is not helpful or constructive to cause parents to think otherwise.

Appendix I

DYSLEXIA

A Different View of Specific Learning Disabilities

My purpose in writing this paper is not so much to emphasise the uselessness of the concept of dyslexia as defined, but to make a case for even greater attention to specific learning disabilities. Apart from producing statistics from my own work, I hope to discuss some of the inherent anomalies implicit in some well-established theories, which we have come to accept uncritically and which continue to stand between us and a clear view of the problem.

Whilst envying those who work in clinical or academic situations their time and resources, field workers have a unique opportunity of meeting this problem as it exists in the community, rather than in a selected population.

The main effort is towards shifting concentration upon unproven causes towards at least an acceptance that this disability may have its origins in cerebral pathology of a most subtle and illusive kind. Until we achieve this, thousands of children, teachers and parents are going to live in the shadow of implied ineptitude, incompetence and mismanagement through no fault of their own.

The walls of classrooms, surgeries and consulting rooms are festooned with the grinning skulls of promises and reassurances to parents that, "he is perfectly all right" or, "he will grow out of it". This is the soft option: the easy way out. Caring parents who are confronted with a child who is failing at school do not seek this kind of protection. If there is a problem they want to know about it so that they can participate in a constructive way towards its solution. They *know* that something is wrong: to be told that there isn't is the one response they cannot cope with. It is this that causes them to despair. To discover that, not only are they left to grapple with the problem on their own, but they are denied the reassurance that the problem can be identified in the first place.

Children, too, should be treated with total honesty. So far as it is within their comprehension, the problems they encounter in learning should be discussed with them. Within this context it is, in my view, not only advisable but obligatory to discuss with them the nature of their disabilities — with a view to their acquiring eventually an objective and unemotional acceptance of their situation. No parent or teacher can do this for them, any more than they can take over from them and work through their difficulties.

Given an honest understanding of their problems and encouragement — plus enlightened help — they will overcome their difficulties and their characters will be all the stronger for it. Cheat them into believing that 'they have no problem', and their eventual disillusionment will destroy far more than their ability to learn.

"Because you don't believe in something, it doesn't cease to exist."

I think the person who said that was talking about God, but it is an equally appropriate rejoinder to any assertion denying a concept which is dependent upon a belief system rather than observed fact.

Dyslexia, apart from being ill-defined, is also dependent upon a belief system and therefore not accessible to proof. Arguments about whether it exists or not are as futile as they are illogical. This is equally true of any concepts which are essentially inferences from behaviour and would certainly include intelligence itself. The fact that we have treated it as an entity, and purported to measure it, does nothing to alter its nature as a quality of behaviour.

This paper does not set out to prove or disprove anything.

135

It is written in an attempt to influence those who are
concerned with the problem of learning difficulties in
children.

A look at some existing views

As Crosby and Liston, *Reading and the Dyslexic Child*, 1968,
page 5 say, in describing dyslexia:

'It appears when a person has impaired visual or auditory perception.'

Unfortunately, they then go on to say:

'A child may have 20/20 vision, but if he has visual imperception
he fails to distinguish between shapes and patterns.'

Not so. It is not this aspect of visual perception which
determines whether a child will have difficulties or not,
but whether he is able to retain his perception in short
term memory.

Similarly, with auditory perception, it is *not* the perception of a simple sequence of two or three digits in the
digit-span test which gives trouble — even the worst affected
seem to manage this — but the inability to retain five plus
digits, (the norm for seven year olds in the Stanford-Binet
Scale).

Op. cit. Chapter 13: Auditory Imperception:

'He could not translate marks on paper into sounds because he
does not correctly *hear* sounds.'

If this were so, a child would not be able to repeat three
digits correctly — as the majority do — but none at all.

Johnson and Myklebust, '67 under the heading Intellectual
Capacities:

'It is our contention that children included in the category of learning disability should have adequate intelligence so that the basis of the homogeneity is a *disability* not an *incapacity*. The question then becomes: How much is adequate? What are the limits within which integrity of intelligence can be assumed and on what measures should these limits be based?'

This may hold in general terms, but it does not hold in the area of mechanical reading we are concerned with:

'Behavioural concomitants of central nervous system functioning begin with perception which is markedly primitive psychologically . . . The neurological condition referred to as agnosia behaviourally may be equivalent to perceptual disorders. The exact psychological and neurological nature of these disturbances is not known, but as suggested by Young's (1964) *Definition of Transducing*, the neurological deficit may consist of inadequate converting of sensations into electrical impulses. This could explain a child being unable to perceive auditorily or visually, the difference between coal and cold etc.'

Most children with specific learning disabilities *can* do this but, their failure beyond this point may well be due, as Young says, to the inadequate converting of sensations into electrical impulses. Also, in the Digit Span test, breakdown may occur where memory has to become imagery – in the sense that, during recall, earlier digits in a series are no longer part of the original auditory sensation, but have to be 'pulled out' from a different locus of the brain.
Op. cit. page 36 Inner Language:

'The intricate aspect of language development is that word meaning must be acquired before words can be used as words' . . . 'Vygotsky (1962) emphasised this feature of language when he stated that a word without meaning was not a word; it is this aspect that we refer to as *inner language*.'

It may be that many children of lower intelligence are

137

not capable of inner language in this sense, and that their reading has to be viewed as essentially meaningless if, as Vygotsky says . . . 'what they produce are not really words but sounds'. My case is that, if the intelligent non-reader could do this, then all would be well with him!

Crosby and Liston op. cit. also discussing 'Meaning':

'Practically all difinitions of reading follow this basic idea that it involves extracting 'meaning' from the printed page.'

I want to suggest that, for the purpose of discussing specific reading disabilities — which have a neurological basis — there is no need to be concerned with 'meaning' or 'understanding'. Comprehension will always be a function of the individual's general intelligence and, if we could bring all children to the level of mechanical reading achieved by some severely mentally handicapped children — some having only extremely limited comprehension — there would be no problem.

The mechanical aspect of reading, therefore, can be viewed as a relatively low grade skill, given the total integrity of the individual's perceptual processes. Durrell, Donald D. 1956, page 42:

'Two background abilities known to be important to begin reading are visual — and auditory — discrimination of word elements. The minimum requirement in the first background ability, that of visual discrimination of word elements, appears to be the ability to match letters . . . The second background ability, that of auditory perception of word elements, is equally important to reading success but somewhat harder to observe and measure. It consists in being able to notice separate signs in spoken words.'

It is not the ability to discriminate visually and auditorily which these children lack — many of them have impressive oral language, and vocabulary at the adult level — what they lack is the ability to retain these perceptions long enough to have utility in the learning process.

Experimental studies on the ITPA (McArthy and Olsen, 1964), suggest that where word or digit stimuli are utilised results of testing are highly intercorrelated.

> 'However, the intercorrelation of auditory memory with the other sub-tests ranged from .06 to .28. It appears that this test emerges as an independent factor in the pattern since its correlation with the rest of the tests is negligible.'

This result argues strongly in favour of viewing short term auditory memory as a peculiar and specific capacity — central to the learning process (particularly of mechanical reading) — and, as yet, imperfectly understood.

This is what makes the supra-analytical approach of the ITPA, Kirk McArthy and Kirk, 1968 somewhat unproductive.

According to the severity of the child's problem, perceptions eventually break down — not because of any deficiency of the numerous elements isolated by many workers e.g. auditory awareness, auditory focus, auditory discrimination etc., but because of his inability to retain a percept more complex than the presentation of two or three digits. It is, fundamentally, a problem of short term memory.

The bogey of minimal brain damage

To state that a child's learning difficulty may be associated with organic factors need not mean that he has a lesion — either congenital or acquired — into which you could put your fist. Unfortunately, the term 'minimal brain damage' or 'dysfunction' which has been commonly used to express this association has an ominous ring to it, particularly for anxious parents.

When the term 'perceptual anomaly' or 'associated with organic factors' is used, it need not have the slightest significance for anything other than the complex processes involved in higher order perception and memory. Indeed, it may be totally wrong to think in terms of any physical lesion and should be viewed as essentially functional — as would be the case, for instance, if a potential were to follow one pathway rather than another.

Understandably, there is a very powerful lobby on the side of the simplest and most palatable explanations. Who wants to subscribe to any degree of neurological impairment when you can account for failure on the grounds of poor teaching?

Crabtree, (*Manchester Guardian*) has, of course, had a peek inside all their heads and established that there is no pathology of any degree with which reading failure in the intelligent child might be associated:

'If I fail, the failure is mine, not his. It is always the teacher's fault, or the parents, if an intelligent child does not learn to read. How could it be otherwise?'

Even the 'hard' neurologists don't go as far as this — they are simply concerned not to diagnose a syndrome or any neurological pathology on the grounds of behavioural signs alone. Some of them appear to be preoccupied with the brain's capacity to compensate and to take over function where certain areas have been destroyed. Clearly this applies in the case of certain orders of behaviour — as in the case of executive speech — but it does not follow that this applies equally where higher order perceptual processes are concerned.

McFee (*Assessment of Organic Impairment*, 1975, page 135)

'The striking specificity of a number of 'developmental' disabilities — (dyslexia, discalculia, spelling difficulties, autism), their parallels with the effects of adult left post-parietal lesions and their frequent co-existence with minor neurological signs and with a history of perinatal difficulty lead one to suspect the presence of a left parietal lesion. The evidence of lack of impairment due to perinatal unilateral lesions leads one to the further conclusion that if there is indeed cerebral damage, it must be bi-lateral.'

In the case of anoxia — which is not uncommon — this would be expected, as oxygen lack in the newborn would be likely to be diffuse in its effect and involve both hemispheres. Only 'traumatic' local lesions would be likely to be unilateral.

The Isle of Wight study

One of the most quoted studies is that of Michael Rutter et al *Education, Health and Behaviour*. This was a survey carried out in the Isle of Wight in 1965 and has the merit of involving a total child population as opposed to a selected one. It did not set out to study the concept of dyslexia in detail but did include a chapter on the neurological aspects of retardation and quite a number of pages are devoted to its consideration. The authors themselves state p.p. 72:

'Only very limited aspects of perception were tested. However, the pattern of WISC verbal performance discrepancies and the largely negative results on constructional tasks are consistent with the view that at 10 years of age inferior form perception and poor visuo-motor skill are less important in relation to reading retardation than are language handicaps (Belmont and Birch 1966). This may not be the case in younger children who are just beginning to read (Benton 1962) and who therefore are having to cope with the initial problems of recognising letters and words. This may be very difficult if their perception of shapes is faulty. On the other hand, in the older child when the meaning of what he reads is all-important, language skills may be more relevant as Benton (1962) has suggested, so that perceptual deficiencies are found in younger retarded readers and conceptual deficiencies in older retarded readers.'

As most of those who recognise specific learning difficulties claim that they are associated primarily with perceptual anomalies, the limited assessment of these skills — particularly that of auditory perception — is unfortunate. The indications are that it is inadequate auditory perception and memory that is the crucial factor in the failure of many of these children. They do not appear even to have isolated this factor as many other workers have done. They go on to quote language development as another important area where delay can be directly associated with low general ability. This may be so, but they do not take account of the fact that among the population of children suffering the most severe and specific reading disabilities, many of them are orally articulate and have impressive oral language and vocabularies well in advance of their age group — frequently at the average adult level.

The survey continues:

'The neurological characteristics of children with intellectual retardation (IQ 70 or less) or with specific reading retardation (reading at least 28 months below the level expected on the basis of a child's age and IQ) are considered.'

They do this in order to compare the neurological characteristics of intellectually retarded children with those of children who have a specific retardation in reading, so that it may be possible to differentiate the nature of general intellectual retardation and specific difficulties in particular educational functions.

If, as I believe, it is established that there is no direct link between the purely mechanical aspect of reading and intelligence, the selection of children on this basis is quite arbitrary. Under the heading 'The meaning of developmental delay' the writers say:

'The presence of deviant neurological characteristics suggests that there is some disorder of brain function. However, it is important to make a clear distinction between definite abnormalities in function and limits or delays in the development of normal functions (Rutter, 1967a, 1969a).'

He goes on to quote spasticity as an example of an abnormality of function:

'It is abnormal at any age and practically always indicates pathology of the central nervous system and usually a structural lesion of the brain.'

It is surely stretching credulity to the limit to suggest that there cannot be any degree of pathology between gross damage, as revealed in spasticity on the one hand, and perfect neurological integrity on the other.

Neurologists are usually commendably conservative but, among those who subscribe to the concept of dyslexia or specific learning difficulties of this type, I know of no claim by any one of them that there is any hard neurological evidence of what is the neurological basis of these anomalies. However, the fact that the evidence comes from psychological tests, or is inferred from behaviour, does not mean that it is any the less neurological in its origin.

Rutter et al go on to say that poor speech or language and severe clumsiness are examples of delays in the development of normal functions.

'These disorders represent extreme variations in normal development rather than the emergence of abnormal patterns. The neonate cannot speak, cannot stand up etc.'

This implication, that all that children with specific learning disabilities have to do is wait and everything will right itself is just not acceptable. For many of them the 'delay' is not made up. They may, as has often been said, compensate for their disabilities — this is particularly so with the more intelligent — but it is dishonest to imply that when these children do acquire literacy it is because they have made up some maturational lag . . .

They again cite the different times of the onset of puberty as an example of how normal development occurs at different rates. They don't go on to consider whether this variation gives rise to widely differing standards of sexual maturity — which of course it does not — but there is a marked difference in the standard of literacy, and the speed at which it is acquired, among those who lack efficient perceptual skills.

They go on:

'There may be extreme delays which are considered disorders because of the severity of the delay and because of associated handicap. These need not be due to any disease or damage to the brain in the ordinary sense of these words.'

Why do they mention disease? Why do they talk about 'damage to the brain'? No one is claiming more for these neurological anomalies than that they are functional and, given the extreme complexity of higher order processes may consist in nothing more than a biochemical absence or defficiency.

'The presence of these developmental delays cannot be taken as sufficient evidence for disease or damage to the brain because the characteristics are entirely normal in younger children and in children of lower mental age.'

Not so. The specific factors concerned in learning disabilities are commonly found and can be demonstrated in children of lower mental age but, more importantly, they cannot be glibly associated with low mental age because many of these children (including ESN[S] children) possess these processes intact and are able to read mechanically.

'In some respects the intellectually retarded child behaves like a much younger normal child. In other words, developmental functions are often related as much to a child's mental age as to his chronological age.'

I repeat, these particular functions are *not* related to the

144

level of intellectual functioning and exist in total isolation from it. Consider again, the very dull child who possesses them intact and the intelligent child who does not.

Intelligence and reading

To have any utility reading must obviously involve receiving some element of meaning from the written word, but the aspect of reading we are concerned with does not involve meaning or understanding and, therefore, does not require any significant degree of intelligence.

Given that specific learning disabilities have their basis in some neurological abnormality, it makes no sense that they are confined to those of average or above average intelligence. I believe the evidence supports the view that whilst low general ability naturally tends to obscure the effects of specific learning disabilities — and makes it more difficult to isolate them — it does not preclude their existence altogether.

In terms of formal learning in the early years children of IQ 75 plus are far less handicapped in the short term, provided their perceptual processes are intact, than the intelligent child who has specific learning disabilities. (Perhaps it is for this reason that many children who are referred to the Schools Psychological Service for the first time relatively late — say in their teens — because of behaviour problems, are found to have low IQs. They have not been referred earlier because of their relatively early reading attainment and the tendency to equate this with intelligence). On the other hand, children of early promise often score less well on later tests simply because the component of learning which inevitably affects later performance and assessment, and which is affected by specific learning disabilities, does not accrue in the normal way.

When using the Stanford-Binet Scale it can happen — and does happen — that in establishing a basal age for an older child using the vocabulary scale, this is found to be beyond year 7 (the first year of the digit span test), and may be, on the basis of the vocabulary score, as high as year 11 or 12. If, when a child is found to fail on digit span at (this) level and a check on his ability at year 7 is carried out, he will often be found to fail. The implications of this for the child's learning failure can be of the utmost significance, apart from its effect on the validity of the IQ.

The Stanford-Binet Scale is a very underrated diagnostic instrument and, although the individual subtests were not intentionally designed to isolate specific disabilities, the memory for designs (visual) and digit span (auditory) seem to do this as well as any subsequent test devised, and better than some.

The Bender Gestalt test, although well established and widely used does not, in fact, measure the all-important factor of retention. It is essentially a copying test and has obvious relevance for the earlier processes of perception but it is not able to indicate the individual's capacity for retaining a configuration in his short term memory.

If, when thinking of intelligence, we view the brain in mechanistic terms the model of the computer is very good and, it may be that for acquiring such skills as mechanical reading an efficient processing system is all that is required.

A brief survey

Over many years, the conclusion became unavoidable that there is a direct connection between difficulty in learning to read and auditory perception and memory as measured by the digit span test. I, intentionally, do not refer to this as auditory sequencing, which is in current usage because the task involves much more than this in its fundamental aspect.

The children referred for learning difficulties in the year 1977/78 amounted to 92. Of these, 43 were identified as suffering from specific learning disabilities. Among the 43, 18 were identified as suffering from defects of mainly visual perception and memory or both visual and auditory perception and memory. The 25 remaining were identified as 'pure' cases of defective auditory perception and memory. An analysis of their reading attainments and their auditory perception and memory — as assessed on digit span — were compared with a control group of 25 children matched for age and sex.

(The repeating of digits backwards is favoured by clinicians and probably has validity for testing impairment of function in adults suffering from disease processes or lesions. In my experience with children, there appears to be no particular significance in the reversed digits test, and, in any event, for some children the repetition of digits forwards presents more than sufficient difficulty.)

Survey Group	Control Group
N = 25	N = 25
Mean digit span 3.6	Mean digit span 4.96
Mean reading age 2.85	Mean reading age 8.53

The chronological ages ranged from 6.4 to 13.1, the mean CA being 9.35 years.

Note

The group contained one boy of 13 years, otherwise the maximum age was 10.4 years.

The digit span test on the Stanford-Binet Scale contains 5 digits at year 7 but for some time it has been my practice to push this assessment to its lower limits and, frequently, individual children have been found to score only 4 or, in some cases, 3 digits. Where the assessments were carried out by a colleague, and this sub-test was failed at the 7 year level, these children have been credited with a score of 4 digits in all cases. This may mean that the mean score of 3.6 for the survey group is significantly higher than it might have been.

In neither group was a reading age of less than 5.9 (Holborn Scale) recorded. There were naturally a number of these among the survey children but, also, there were three such children in the Control Group. As the mean was arrived at by using an N of 25 in each case, the mean reading age is depressed for this reason.

Control Group

An interesting feature which emerged in the control group was that in certain cases a significantly high reading age was found to occur together with a considerable facility in the digit span test e.g:

Sex	Age	Digit Span	RA
M	7yrs 7mths	6	9yrs
M	9yrs	6	11yrs 4mths
M	9yrs 4mths	6	10yrs 10mths
M	10yrs	6	11yrs 4mths

The converse was also found to obtain e.g:

Sex	Age	Digit Span	RA
M	7yrs 10mths	4	6yrs 10mths
M	9yrs	4	5yrs 9mths
M	8yrs 6mths	4	6yrs 9mths

Survey Group

In the survey group, the same association between poor auditory perception and memory and low reading attainment was found and, additionally, with these children, IQ scores were, of course, available. Some significant examples were:

Sex	Age	Digit Span	IQ	RA
M	8yrs 4mths	3	85	Non reader
M	10yrs	3	Average	6.6
M	8yrs 5mths	3	95	6.5
M	7yrs 7mths	3	94	Non reader
M	10yrs	3	120	7.0

With limited time I did some cross checking and asked one First School to let me see some of its young readers. Three

148

were sent to me, who produced the following results:

Sex	Age	RA	Digit Span
M	5.6	7.3	4
M	6.0	9.0	5
F	6.1	6.3	5

As the reading of the five-year-old is impressive, it suggests that the achievement of four digits at this age is indicative of basically very efficient perceptual processes.

Additionally, some children known to be good readers were seen at an ESN(M) school with the following results:

Sex	CA	Digit Span	IQ	RA
F	13 yrs	5	70	13 +
F	10 yrs	5	67	9 yrs 3 mths
F	11 yrs 5 mths	5	71	9 yrs 9 mths
F	11 yrs 11 mths	6	64	10 yrs 9 mths

It follows that, if this hypothesis is supported by sufficient evidence, that mechanical reading ability in children is a direct function of auditory perception *as tested by a repetition of digits* – this offers a means of establishing, at an early age, whether or not a child is at risk in this sense. On balance, I am relatively pessimistic about the prognosis for these children, particularly about those who are less able. As has been said before, the very able child can and does resort to all manner of means to circumvent his difficulties but I do *not* believe as some workers (Rutter et al) suggest, that it is essentially developmental and that they somehow 'grow out of it'. As the persistence of these difficulties into adulthood suggest, it is more probable that the basic condition is irreversible and something the individual has to learn to live with – sometimes successfully, sometimes not.

It may be that we have to reappraise the whole question of cognitive assessment and, by so doing identify two important groups. Firstly, those who score well on traditional tests in the early years, yet show a pronounced difficulty with auditory perception (as tested by Digit Span) — these are the ones who need early and intensive help because their learning potential is significantly threatened.

Secondly, those children who may achieve modest intelligence quotients but who can be identified as possessing good perceptual skills; these are children who will do relatively well educationally, and whose formal attainments will be good relative to their general ability.

This is the group with whom remedial teachers have impressive success: the first group contain many of the more intractible problems which have defeated some very able teachers.

Appendix II

COMMENTS ON SOME RECENT VIEWS ON LEARNING

One of the best discussions of recent years is to be found in *School Learning Mechanisms and Behaviour* (R.J. Riding, Open Books 1980).

In discussing the psychological evidence for short-term memory Riding, in my view, draws the wrong conclusions.

In discussing Moss and Sharac's experiment to investigate the stages of processing of newly received information (1970) he states:

'An implication of these experiments is that new information is passed from sensory memory into Short Term Memory where it is analysed before being transferred into Long Term Memory. This analysis takes several seconds and while it is undertaken the information is very vulnerable to loss either by the reception of further material or by the introduction into Short Term Memory of distracting thoughts from Long Term Memory. It is therefore important that a child in a listening situation has sufficient time to process the speech bit by bit as it is received, otherwise the sense of some of the sentences will be lost and his understanding of the whole will be incomplete. In considering the individual differences between learners in their ability to receive information, it should be stressed that a child who has difficulty in understanding information probably does so because his Short Term Memory analysis system is inefficient and hence slow. It seems very unlikely that it is due to his Short Term Memory store being physically smaller than those of his more able colleagues.'

151

It cannot be stressed too strongly that many children who are failing to acquire literacy can and do learn from information received orally. They have no problem in processing and assimilating meaningful material in the form of the spoken word.

I am quoting from Riding at length because he states succinctly the possible locus of the problem, yet at the same time appears to demonstrate what I believe is a basic and common misconception of its nature, and how, precisely, it affects children's learning.

> 'It appears then, that for both visual and auditory input the information remains active in the sensory memory for a few seconds after it has been received. The role of the sensory memory appears to be to hold information long enough for it be be transferred to short term memory. For both stores (iconic and echoic) loss can be caused by (1) decay with time and (2) masking by further incoming stimuli; more images or sounds. No work has been reported on individual differences in sensory memory;' *could it be that a child with learning or reading difficulties is deficient in his sensory memory capacity.*

What Riding does not suggest, but which I believe to be a fundamental determinant of the learning capacity (of symbolic material) for some children, is that the LOSS is determined by constitutional factors of a very subtle kind.

Thus, what he refers to as sensory memory capacity is better conceived as a perceptual capacity, on the premise that it is not tenable to use the term memory until something has been recorded — however long or short-term that recording might be.

Before something can be forgotten, it has to have been learned. Teachers sometimes make assumptions that a child has learned something when, in fact, it is not the case. It may have been only partially learned, and does not exist in any form which is stable and enduring — which is an essential condition if it is to have any utility in a formal learning situation.

Again, discussing short-term memory (STM) Riding states:

'New information in sensory memory is transmitted to STM where it is analysed ready for storage in LTM. Evidence for the existence of STM comes from analogy with computers, physiological findings and psychological research.

The Limitation of Input

A basic experience in learning is that we can accept a limited input. If for instance, you dictate a string of digits to a person and ask him to recall them (try it on someone, seven digits: $4 - 7 - 2 - 8 - 5 - 1 - 6$ and again with nine digits: $9 - 3 - 7 - 1 - 8 - 6 - 5 - 0 - 4$) you observe that he or she finds it difficult consistently to receive a string of more than seven. On the other hand given a few presentations we can learn much longer strings (many telephone numbers are nine digits long). It is readily apparent that while input is limited, the total capacity of all that we can remember is very large . . . '

There is a danger that two totally erroneous inferences might be drawn from this. Firstly, that this limiting mechanism is universal, and that it varies only slightly in degree as between one (normal) individual and another and, secondly, that it is a capacity which is responsive to training and can be developed.

Dealing with the first point: it is clear that many children are handicapped by reason of a severe limitation on input of this type and that it is this that curtails their ability to process symbolic material and to learn to read. But limitation of this degree is not universal. The disabled (in this sense) child, can process only a small fraction of the 'input' of this type as compared with his peers. While they, the normal, demonstrate what might well be a universal 'limiting' mechanism, it is not of an order as will impede their learning. They will use their unimpaired and adequate

153

capacity for such processing to good account and, hopefully, be efficient learners. The perceptually disabled child is unable to do this. He has two 'limiting' mechanisms: one universal, and one very much his own! Secondly, whatever may be the case with adults, there is mounting evidence that this capacity is peculiarly resistant to training in children.

It may be that some adults gradually acquire a greater facility for dealing with numbers in the way Riding says over the years, but I would doubt that it occurs in cases where the disability is severe. (See case histories.) Some successful adults will admit to a continuing and frustrating difficulty with numbers, particularly telephone numbers, even though they are able to take a detached and unemotional view of their problem. Children in this predicament on the other hand cannot take a sophisticated or mature view of their situation and are inevitably more disturbed by it, both directly, as it affects their learning, and indirectly, through their emotional reaction to frustration and failure.

Riding appears to assume that all children proceed to learn following the model he describes without encountering any major perceptual problems on the way.

His model STM − LTM − Meaning, is possibly over-simplified, taking insufficient account of the complexities of higher perceptual processes.

If all goes well at the STM level, transfer to LTM and accommodation as he calls it are straightforward processes. The breakdown, if any, occurs at the STM level, and, until perception is complete at this level there can be no question of transfer − except of gobbledegook.

Riding's STM has to be viewed as essentially a part of the process of perception: it is misleading to think of it in any other terms.

He goes on to suggest that,

'In terms of learning difficulty it is probable that children whose learning performance is inferior to the typical for their age have failed adequately to acquire the appropriate processing skills.'

I agree with this statement, but it is possible to have a different view of the processing skills he refers to, and where precisely in the cognitive hierarchy they are to be found. He sees them as a part of the learning process: I see them as essentially a part of the perceptual process — before any learning can be said to be taking place.

He does not appear to take account of the impressive learning of some children who are obviously capable of learning and assimilating oral information, yet cannot process symbolic material in the way he appears to assume they can. If these children can learn successfully from verbal instructions, what processing has taken place is of a different order. Their problem is not with the processing of meaningful information but with, for them, the peculiarly inaccessible information implicit in the written word.

In discussing the possible improvement of processing performance Riding refers to Kinsbourne and Cohen's (1971) study comparing the performance of Israeli and English subjects of consonant memory span and digit span. The Israeli subjects were found to be better with consonants, which they attributed to their experience with Hebrew vowel-less script. He suggests that this hints at the possibility of improving processing performance by training. However, he recognises that a basic problem is that these processes do not appear to be under the learner's conscious control and goes on to say: 'It is not that processing is not learned, but once it is learned it is automatically employed whenever stimuli are presented.'

Here Riding seems to be equating such stimuli as digits with qualitatively quite different 'meaningful' material. Many children with specific processing problems have no difficulty with this type of material: they are, as has been said, often efficient learners in this regard. Although Riding's words are only 'hints at the possibility . . . ' it is difficult to see that this study reveals any new evidence that this specific component of the perceptual process is directly responsive to training. Would that it were! When, as is the case with a minority of

155

children it is seriously inadequate or defective, it does appear to be peculiarly intractible and resistant to modification.

If such children do eventually succeed in partially mastering the decoding skill, it is my submission that they do this by using alternative strategies, possibly in the way that (say) the profoundly deaf have to do, and not because they have succeeded in developing the skill in the normal way.

This, together with the evidence discussed earlier, further suggests that this particular skill — or more correctly capacity — is either innate, or has had functional limits set on it through constitutional factors.

GLOSSARY

Included in this glossary are some words which are not to be found in the text. They are included because they sometimes occur in parents' discussions with teachers or other specialists.

a- A negative prefix — as in aphasia — loss of speech as a result of cerebral accident or disease.

AETIOLOGY Cause or origin of disease.

ALEXIA Loss of ability to read — due to accident or disease. To be contrasted with dyslexia.

APRAXIA Difficulty in performing motor (hand) movements — as a result of or associated with disease or accident to the central nervous system.

AUDITORY PERCEPTION The central organisation and interpretation of sense data received through the ear. The process has to be completed before perception can be said to have occurred.

CENTRAL NERVOUS SYSTEM The brain with the spinal cord — as distinct from sensory nerves.

CEREBRAL DOMINANCE The theory that in most people one hemisphere of the brain is dominant in the control of body movement — the left hemisphere in the case of right-handed people (the majority), and the right hemisphere in the case of left-handed people. Generally the left hemisphere controls language function. In some cases dominance is not well established and this is held to be associated with certain disorders of speech and learning (particularly reading) problems.

COGNITION To do with all the forms of knowing — hence perceiving, remembering, thinking, reasoning are all forms of cognition. Cognitive tests — such as intelligence tests — involve these processes.

CONGENITAL Existing or present at birth — such as diseases or defects. Sometimes, but not always inherited.

DYSLEXIA An ambiguous word, never satisfactorily defined. (The prefix dys- from the Greek DYS meaning bad). It is generally used to refer to a reading disability of constitutional origin. In the case of a similar disability affecting writing, the appropriate word would be DYSGRAPHIA.

DYSGRAPHIA Inability or difficulty to perform the movements required for handwriting. It usually has a neurological basis.

DYSCALCULIA Inability or severe difficulty to use numbers. The numerical equivalent of dyslexia and therefore having a neurological or constitutional basis.

ELECTROENCEPHALOGRAPH (EEG) The recording of the electrical activity of the cerebral cortex of the brain.

ENDOGENOUS A condition or defect of hereditary or genetic origin and therefore existing from birth.

EXOGENOUS A condition or defect which is not associated with constitutional factors but has its origins in incidents or conditions in the environment.

EXTRANEOUS Outside of: not belonging to.

FUNCTIONAL Not structural or organic but to do with the operation or function of the organ or capacity concerned.

GRAPHEME The written symbol representing a word or sound.

HARD NEUROLOGICAL SIGNS Evidence of malfunction or pathology of the nervous system recognised by neurologists in the diagnosis of disease.

HYPERKINESIS Excessive motor movement. Commonly and sometimes incorrectly used to describe very active children. It is only appropriate when behaviour is excessively restless and usually non-directed.

INCIDENTAL LEARNING Learning which takes place as part of general life experience and not as a result of formal instruction in the classroom.

INNATE Inborn.

LANGUAGE Means of expression and communication generally employing words, but not always. Recently there has been interest in communication through bodily disposition and movement which are held to signal important non-verbal responses and attitudes.

LEARNING DISABILITY An ambiguous term sometimes used synonymously with learning difficulty. In this book the clear distinction is made that a disability is associated with constitutional factors — however slight — while a learning difficulty refers to learning problems without such association.

LEXICAL To do with words.

LINGUISTICS The study of the nature and function of language.

MATURATION All that part of development which is not dependent upon learning. The process of natural growth to maturity.

MATURATIONAL LAG A slowness in the processes of maturation — particularly in neurological organisation and development.

MEMORY The general ability to store and recall previously experienced sensations and perceptions when the stimulus that originally evoked them is no longer present.

MINIMAL BRAIN DAMAGE A confusing and misused concept. See text.

MIXED LATERALITY The performance of some acts with a right-side preference and others with the left. See CEREBRAL DOMINANCE.

MODALITY The channels through which information is received in formal learning. These are mainly visual (seeing), and auditory (hearing).

MORPHEME The smallest unit capable of bearing meaning in language.

OPERATIONAL See FUNCTIONAL.

PERCEPTION The complex process of organising and interpreting information coming into the brain via the sense organs so as to give it utility and meaning.

PERCEPTUAL CONSTANCY The ability to perceive the invariant properties of objects — such as shape and size — in spite of a change in the disposition of these objects in space, and the differing impressions they make on the sense organs.

PERCEPTUAL DISABILITY A disorder or defect in the processes of perception which inhibits or prevents efficient interpretation of sensory information.

PERCEPTUO-MOTOR Refers to the interaction of the different channels of perception with motor activity.

PHONEME The smallest unit of sound in language.

PHONICS In the teaching of reading; the association of the sound (phoneme) with its written symbol (grapheme).

PSYCHOLINGUISTICS A relatively new study of the psychology of language and the process of communication through its use.

READABILITY LEVEL An indication of the difficulty of reading material by reference to reading age.

READING AGE Generally the age level at which a child is reading mechanically. It does not take account of comprehension.

RECEPTIVE LANGUAGE Written or spoken language for communication to others. The receptive language skills are listening and reading, and many non-readers are efficient and successful listeners.

SENSORI-MOTOR Refers to the association between information coming in via the sense organs and its translation into appropriate responses in motor behaviour.

SOFT NEUROLOGICAL SIGNS Evidence of neurological abnormalities which are too slight to be picked up in the course of standard neurological examination. They may be discernable only in the individual's performance on tests involving perception and other aspects of cognitive behaviour. They are of interest to the psychologist who studies behaviour as opposed to basic neurological function.

STREPHOSYMBOLIA The reversal of letters or words in perception: p for b or was for saw etc. The 'twisted symbols' often referred to in the history of dyslexia.

SYNTAX The structure of language with its grammar and rules — as in the sentences of English with their objects and verbs.

TACTILE PERCEPTION The interpretation of information received via the sense of touch. An excellent and specialised example is the use of Braille.

UTILITY Usefulness, of sensory or other organ function. Primary biological utility refers to the preservation of life or the species.